FIGHTING FROM THE HEAVENS

Tactics and Training of USAAF Bomber Crews, 1941–45

CHRIS MCNAB

CASEMATE
Philadelphia & Oxford

Published in the United States of America and Great Britain in 2023 by
CASEMATE PUBLISHERS
1950 Lawrence Road, Havertown, PA 19083, USA
and
The Old Music Hall, 106–108 Cowley Road, Oxford OX4 1JE, UK

Hardcover Edition: ISBN 978-1-63624-382-5
Digital Edition: ISBN 978-1-63624-383-2

A CIP record for this book is available from the British Library

Printed and bound in the United Kingdom by CPI Group (UK) Ltd, Croydon, CR0 4YY
Typeset in India by DiTech Publishing Services

For a complete list of Casemate titles, please contact:

CASEMATE PUBLISHERS (US)
Telephone (610) 853-9131
Fax (610) 853-9146
Email: casemate@casematepublishers.com
www.casematepublishers.com

CASEMATE PUBLISHERS (UK)
Telephone (0)1226 734350
Email: casemate-uk@casematepublishers.co.uk
www.casematepublishers.co.uk

Cover image: A combat crew receives final instructions just before taking off in a mighty YB-17 bomber from a bombardment squadron base at the field, Langley Field, Va. (Photographer: Alfred T. Palmer; Office of War Information color slides and transparencies collection, Library of Congress)

Contents

Introduction   iv

1   Recruitment and Training   1
2   Pilot and Copilot   15
3   Bombardier   57
4   Navigator and Radio Operator   91
5   Gunners   123
6   Flight Engineer   165
7   Operational Challenges   189

Sources   213

Introduction

Freely available online, readers can find a collection of instructional German wartime gun-camera footage, showing how German fighter aircraft should attack the streams of American bombers hammering the Third Reich on an almost daily basis. Although the footage was filmed for training purposes for fighter pilots in 1943–44, to modern eyes it is a haunting vision of the realities of aerial combat. The grainy black-and-white clips, each lasting little more than 30 seconds, show B-17 Flying Fortress and B-24 Liberator bombers being slashed and broken from various angles, cannon shells ripping into wings and fuselages, Plexiglas turrets shattering, engines exploding and streaming with fire. Inside each of the aircraft, 10 men fought for their lives, desperately attempting to preserve their metal world, the only thing shielding them from the 200mph+ sub-zero airstream outside, or holding them above a fatal, horribly centrifugal, 3–5-mile plunge to earth.

Many, many U.S. Army Air Forces (USAAF) bomber crews did not make it home. The U.S. Eighth Air Force, for example, suffered about half of the entire USAAF casualties during World War II, with more than 26,000 dead and 28,000 men becoming prisoners of war. In total, 10,561 aircraft of the "Mighty Eighth" were shot down. This includes both bombers and fighters, but—to give a sense of the bomber cost—4,754 aircraft of this total were B-17s alone.

During the early stages of the strategic bombing campaign against Germany from 1942, there was a bomber crew casualty rate in excess of 80 percent. The bravery required to climb repeatedly aboard a bomber aircraft, knowing with near certainty that at some point that aircraft would either be shot down or severely damaged, can only be imagined.

Some individual missions would go down as dark historical monuments to the horrors of modern air warfare. On October 14, 1943, for example, 291 USAAF bombers went to attack the ball-bearing works at Schweinfurt in Bavaria. The initial fighter cover from P-47 Thunderbolts had to turn back well short of the target because of range limitations. The bombers, and the 2,900 men aboard them, were attacked by swarms of motivated and professional German fighters for hours on end. Hundreds of antiaircraft guns threw up lethal walls of steel and high explosive, through which the bombers had to fly straight and level on their bomb run, a gift for well-trained enemy gun crews. In total, 60 of the bombers would be shot down, with 600 airmen becoming casualties over enemy territory—dead, wounded, prisoner. An additional 17 bombers made it back to England but crash-landed and were written off, while another 122 aircraft required significant repairs to keep them flying. With a 21 percent crew casualty rate, the battle was one of the costliest individual bombing raids of the war. There are many other examples of near equal or even greater levels of cost. Operation *Tidal Wave*—the low-level bombing of oil refineries around Ploesti, Romania, by aircraft of the Ninth Air Force on August 1, 1943—saw 177 B-24s deployed, but 53 were destroyed and 55 damaged, with 310 aircrew dead or missing and another 190 captured.

Strategic bombing

In grim balance to the toll inflicted by the enemy upon USAAF bombers, the American crews truly unleashed hell upon those below. Keeping our focus on the Eighth Air Force, the bombers of VIII Bomber Command flew more than 440,000 sorties and pounded Germany or German-occupied territories with some 697,000 tons of bombs. At the peak of the air campaign's scale and efficiency, the Eighth Air Force could put 2,000 heavy bombers into the air for a single daylight mission, eventually (and much to the relief of the crews) with all-round mission fighter escort from P-51 Mustangs, P-47 Thunderbolts, and P-38 Lightnings fitted with drop tanks.

Working in rotation with Royal Air Force (RAF) night-bombing raids as part of the Combined Bomber Offensive from early 1943, the USAAF aircraft in Europe literally wiped entire city districts from the map. The scale of the raids grew to dizzying heights of destructive force. On March 18, 1945, for example, the Eighth Air Force sent up 1,329 heavy bombers and 733 fighters to strike northern Germany, the bulk of the raid directed towards Berlin. The stream of heavy bombers released more than 3,000 tons of bombs over the city, killing an estimated 3,000 civilians. Just a month previously, USAAF bombers had delivered their payload alongside that of the RAF to produce the near-total destruction of Dresden, one of the most controversial acts of strategic bombing in the war, killing around 25,000 civilians. (Hamburg had received similar attention in July 1943.) But even this mighty act of obliteration was dwarfed by some of the air raids directed against Japan in 1945, flown by B-29 Superfortresses from XXI Bomber Command, part of the Twentieth Air Force in the Pacific Theater of Operations

B-24 liberators of the Fifteenth Air Force strike the Concordia Vega oil refinery, Ploesti, Romania, on May 31, 1944, keeping formation through heavy flak. (LOC)

(PTO). In the single most destructive conventional air raid of the war, Operation *Meetinghouse* on the night of March 9/10, 1945, 279 B-29s deposited tens of thousands of incendiaries over Tokyo, the resulting firestorm destroying nearly 16 square miles of the city and killing as many as 100,000 of its citizens. USAAF bombers also delivered the war-ending atomic bombs over Hiroshima and Nagasaki the following August, although by then there was actually little destructive difference between the conventional raids and the atomic attacks.

The bomber crews

The USAAF bomber crews who fought in World War II were, as is invariably the way in war, scarcely out of their childhood years. The age of a typical USAAF bomber crew was just 19–25 years old. But the responsibility heaped upon them, and the mental endurance expected of them, was almost unimaginable when viewed from the more protective instincts of our modern age. They flew and fought as an integrated crew, individuals welded into a single entity by shared experiences of combat and a heavy weight of cooperative responsibility, with the survival of every crew member dependent on the stoic efficiency of the others. If one man failed in his duty or his responsibility—as the manuals quoted in this book often point out—it could at best jeopardize the successful completion of the mission (the entire reason the crew had put itself at risk) or at worst contribute towards the destruction of the aircraft and its occupants.

Crew sizes and roles differed according to the type of bomber aircraft. In this book we focus our attention on multi-engine bombers, excluding single-engine types such as dive-bombers and torpedo bombers. At the diminutive end of the scale were light bombers such as the Douglas A-26 Invader, essentially a twin-engine ground-attack aircraft with a three-man crew: pilot, navigator/bombardier/radio operator, and gunner (the latter moving between dorsal and ventral turrets). Then came the medium bombers, again twin-engine aircraft but with heavier payloads, longer range, and better altitude capabilities—prime wartime examples of the type include the Douglas A-20 Havoc, Martin B-26 Marauder, and North American B-25 Mitchell. Crew numbers of medium bombers ranged between three and seven. A B-26G Marauder, for example, had a pilot, copilot, bombardier/radio operator, navigator/radio operator, and three gunners.

At the summit of bomber power, however, were the "heavies": four-engine, long-range types with mighty bombloads and bristling defensive armament. The defining USAAF heavy bombers of World War II were the Boeing B-17 Flying Fortress, the Boeing B-29 Superfortress, and the Consolidated B-24 Liberator. The Flying Fortress and the Liberator both came with 10-man crews. The B-17G, for example, had the following crew members: pilot, copilot, navigator, bombardier/nose gunner, flight engineer/top turret gunner, radio operator, two waist gunners, a ball turret gunner, and a tail gunner. The B-29—the most sophisticated of the wartime bombers—had an 11-man crew, the composition partly reflecting the advanced technologies aboard: pilot, copilot, bombardier, flight engineer, navigator, radio operator, radar observer, right gunner, left gunner, central fire control operator, and tail gunner.

This book gives an insight into the various crew positions using excerpts from many USAAF wartime manuals, with interspersed first-hand accounts of actual combat putting some human flesh on the technical bones. From an organizational point of view, there are, naturally, clear distinctions between each of the roles—pilots flew the aircraft, copilots assisted in flying duties, navigators provided route planning and guidance, bombardiers aimed and delivered the ordnance, flight engineers kept the electrical and mechanical systems functioning, gunners fired at enemy fighters, and so on. But the manuals make equally clear that each crew member's role blurred operationally into that of every other man aboard. For a start, crew members frequently multi-tasked during an operation, either through designated responsibilities or because another crew member had been wounded. Bombardiers, flight engineers, and radio operators would act as gunners, copilots might take over as bombardiers, gunners would assist in flight engineer duties. Cooperation and communication were constant. The navigator, for example, would provide the pilot and copilot with route guidance to the objective; the bombardier worked with the pilot and copilot to make the correct bomb run; the flight engineer prepared bomb doors and ordnance for dropping; the gunners reported fighter attacks and bomb rack malfunctions; the radio operator gave everyone streams of relevant flight information. The bomber crew functioned as an organic whole, using their cooperative intelligence to turn an aircraft into a purposeful combat machine.

All of the manuals here presented are technical in nature, requiring detailed knowledge of systems and procedures to be converted into pressure-tested automaticity in combat. The educational level of air crew was therefore higher than many other branches of service; pre-service education in math, applied sciences, and practical engineering were welcomed. But at the same time, the air crews needed to be of exceptional mental strength. Up until 1944, bomber crews were required to complete 25 missions to complete their tour of duty (it was later raised to 30 then 35 missions), but they had only about a 30–50 percent chance of surviving to that total, depending on the period of the war. Physical conditions on the flights were punishing in the extreme. Missions over Europe might last as little as two hours or as much as ten hours, while those in the Pacific could extend up to 16 hours for the long-range B-29 strikes.

A side view of the twin-engine Douglas A-26 Invader, which had a crew of three and served as a light bomber and ground-attack aircraft. (Eric Friedebach CC BY-SA 2.0)

While the B-29 had the luxury of a pressurized and heated cabin, most of the medium and heavy bombers had no such comforts, thus the air crew would spend the hours sat on hard seats in cramped metal spaces, freezing in temperatures as low as −50 degrees F, relying on oxygen masks to keep them from passing out and heated flying suits to prevent their lapse into hyperthermia. Technologies often failed, however, and crew members might suddenly float into unconsciousness or even death from anoxia, while others suffered frostbite in their extremities. (One common problem was gunners having their hands glue themselves to freezing gun metal after they removed their gloves to clear weapon stoppages.) If they needed to urinate, they would do so in bags; defecation was either avoided altogether or simply done inside the clothes.

Despite these conditions, the bomber crew would have to perform a multitude of mental and technical challenges, efficiently and constantly. Then they would have to cope with the very professional efforts of the enemy to destroy them. Literally dozens, sometimes hundreds, of enemy fighters would swarm around them, firing streams of machine-gun and cannon projectiles into wings and fuselages, sometimes leaving nothing more than a few holes, other times igniting fuel tanks and bombs, destroying engines, or ripping off a wing or tailplane. Flak would pepper the sky and puncture airframes, over the toughest targets exploding in what appeared to be unsurvivable densities. Bomber crews would literally see nearby aircraft blown to pieces or go spiraling down in sickening spins. They would feel their aircraft stagger under blows of enemy fire, and feel the terrifying inrush of super-cold, super-fast air as the holes widened. Many would have to take to the parachute, leaping out of dying aircraft knowing that if they survived the drop, they would land in a city they had just bombed, full of vengeful citizens.

The manuals included here are, to varying degrees, dry and patriotic, aiming to instill skill and confidence in the crew members and not fear and uncertainty. But they are, at the same time, deadly serious about what faced the airman in contested skies. The authors of the manuals understood that the very best chances of survival for these thousands of men would be to know themselves, their aircraft, their responsibilities, and their other crew members better than they knew their own families, far behind and below them.

CHAPTER I

Recruitment and Training

With the United States' full entry into World War II in December 1941, the USAAF, like all branches of the U.S. military, faced the immediate need for rapid expansion in both men and materiel. The spectacular scale at which it achieved this goal is indicated by the fact that in 1939, as war flared up in Europe, the U.S. Army Air Corps (USAAC)—the organizational predecessor of the USAAF—consisted of 20,000 personnel and 2,400 aircraft, many of the latter obsolete. By its peak in 1944, by contrast, the USAAF had 2.4 million personnel and 80,000 of the world's most modern aircraft.

The bomber arm of the USAAF required well-trained crews, and training took time, especially for the more technically challenging roles in the aircraft—pilot, copilot, bombardier, navigator, and flight engineer. In the case of a pilot, for example, some 36 weeks of training lay ahead to take him from raw recruit to advanced pilot standard. This might sound like a lot but given the spectrum of demands on a bomber combat pilot the pace of instruction was actually dauntingly brisk, especially as many of the new recruits had never even flown in an aircraft before, let alone piloted one. During the basic training phase, a pilot would be conducting solo flights after just six hours of flight instruction. Naturally, the USAAF was eager to recruit those who already had civilian flight experience. The enlistment in 1941 of one of the most famous bomber pilots of World War II—the Hollywood actor James Stewart—was certainly helped by the fact that he held a private pilot's license, this balancing out the fact that he was almost too thin and too old for air crew training.

After an initially slow start in 1939–41, the USAAF bomber training program became exceptionally productive, graduating 27,000 heavy bombardment,

6,000 medium bombardment and 1,600 light bombardment crews between December 1942 and August 1945. For B-17 and B-24 heavy bombers, the primary training formation from 1942–43 was the Second Air Force and its Operational Training Units (OTUs); from mid-1943 other air forces began to incorporate training programs to meet the sheer demand for personnel across a breadth of theaters. (Medium and light bombardment training fell to the Third Air Force.) Crew training was divided into three overarching phases. Phase 1 provided instruction to each crew member in their intended specialty (pilot, navigator, gunner etc.), while in Phase 2 the individuals were brought together in a single aircraft to train as a team for operations. Phase 3 coordinated multiple crews for unit training, conducting simulated missions from briefing to return to base. The training program was far from perfect, troubled across the war by shortages of aircraft, equipment, and logistics, with complaints from frontline units that new air crew often had little mastery of their core skills. The program did, however, ensure the United States was able to prosecute its strategic bombing campaign on a massive scale.

Aviation Cadet Training for the Army Air Forces was published in 1943 in an effort to draw more and more people into USAAF air crew, at a time when the growing Allied strategic bombing campaign in Europe was hungrily soaking up tens of thousands of new recruits. It clearly explains who the USAAF wanted to recruit as air crew, what roles lay open to them, and the training journey ahead. It also hints at the fact the recruiters are looking for people made of the "right stuff"—mental acuity and emotional resilience were far more important than mere physical fitness. One point of nomenclature needs clarification. Although the USAAC had effectively been replaced by the USAAF by March 1942, the Air Corps remained a combat arm classification until 1947, hence the references to it here.

★★★

From *Aviation Cadet Training for the Army Air Forces* (1943)
COMMAND OF THE AIR IS VITAL TO VICTORY

We are in the midst of the most momentous war of modern times. A coalition of powerful and ruthless enemies seeks not only to overwhelm us but to annihilate our institutions and our civilization. They have struck with suddenness and with all the force at their command and have shown that it is their aim to conquer swiftly and completely. Therefore, we have no time to lose. We must surpass them in both strength and speed of attack. We must press them back behind their own borders and there defeat them so decisively that they can never again attempt to impose their wills and their ways of life on a people who cherish liberty above all things; a people always willing to lay down their lives to preserve their freedom.

The United States is now engaged in the greatest aircraft production program ever undertaken by any country. That program, however, can be translated into air supremacy only if we can muster the qualified manpower to keep our planes flying. And the source of this manpower lies in the youth of the land—they are the men who will "Keep 'em Flying!"

Youth alone has the physical fitness, the mental alertness, the personal daring to meet the acid test for air crews of high-powered military aircraft.

Our Nation's future depends upon command of the air. The future of freedom and liberty everywhere is in the hands of our youth.

Aviation Cadet Training for the ARMY AIR FORCES

By agreement between the Army and the Navy, important changes in procedure of induction into the Armed Forces have been effected, which now make it possible for young men to volunteer for air crew training.

This new procedure again offers the privilege of choice of service, limited, however, to men who are physically and otherwise qualified to meet the high standards required for Aviation Cadet training.

Men between the ages or 18 and 26, inclusive, may apply through voluntary induction for air crew training to become bombardiers, navigators, and pilots.

Young men who have reached the age of 17 but have not yet attained their eighteenth birthday may apply for enlistment in the Air Corps Enlisted Reserve.

How to Apply for Air Crew Training

This is how a young man can find out whether or not he can fly and fight in an aviation branch of the Armed Forces:

1. Go to any Aviation Cadet Examining Board (usually located in the Post Office or Federal Building in important cities and also at most Air Forces stations) and apply for examination. This examination will consist of two parts: (a) mental, and (b) physical. If the applicant passes the examination, he will be given a letter addressed to the commanding officer of the Armed Forces Induction Station, stating that he is considered to be qualified mentally and physically for air crew training to become a pilot, navigator, or bombardier. This letter, to be utilized as evidence of the Aviation Cadet Examining Board's certification of the eligibility of the applicant, must be presented to the commanding officer of an induction station within forty-five days from its date of issue. The letter becomes invalid, however, if the applicant is called for induction in his regular order number by his Selective Service Board before he is accepted for voluntary induction.
2. Go to his Selective Service Board and volunteer for induction. (No applicant can volunteer for induction after he has been called in his regular order number for induction by his Selective Service Board.) If he is accepted as a volunteer for induction, the Selective Service Board will send him to an Armed Forces Induction Station for induction into the Army of the United States.
3. At the Armed Forces Induction Station, present the letter from the Aviation Cadet Examining Board addressed to the Commanding Officer, Armed Forces Induction Station.

Upon induction the applicant will be assigned to a Technical Training Command Basic Training Center for processing, after which he will be sent to a selected college for a five-month course of preparatory pre-flight training. The academic portion of this course will comprise mathematics, physics, geography, modern history, and English. An applicant whose educational qualifications are such as to make unnecessary the preparatory academic training course may be exempted from it; in which case he will be sent from the Technical Command Basic Training Center to an Army Air Forces Classification Center for testing and classification. There he will be given comprehensive psychological and physical examinations to determine in detail his aptitude for bombardier, navigator, or pilot training. If he passes these tests successfully, he will be appointed an Aviation Cadet and sent to an Air Forces Training Center to begin the type of air crew training for which he appears best adapted. If, however, the tests indicate that he does not possess sufficient aptitude or is not qualified physically tor air crew training, he will not be appointed an Aviation Cadet, but will be assigned to another type of training.

Young men of 17 and less than 18 years of age may also apply for Aviation Cadet air crew training. The procedure is as follows:

1. Obtain written consent of parents for enlistment in the Air Corps Enlisted Reserve.
2. Go to an Aviation Cadet Examining Board and apply for examination and enlistment.

If the applicant is found to be mentally, morally and physically qualified, he will be enlisted in the Air Corps Enlisted Reserve by the Aviation Cadet Examining Board. He will be on an inactive status and may continue his education or civilian pursuits until he is 18, at which time, or as soon thereafter as practicable, he will be called to active duty for preparatory pre-flight training. He may, at the time of enlistment, have the option of designating the month between his eighteenth birthday and six months thereafter in which he desires to be called to active duty. If, upon reaching the age of 18, he is a college or a high school student, his call to active duty may be deferred upon his request until the end of his current semester, provided that it is completed not later than six months after his eighteenth birthday.

Qualifications and Eligibility

General. —An applicant for appointment as Aviation Cadet for air crew training must have reached his eighteenth birthday but not have reached his twenty-seventh birthday.

An applicant for enlistment in the Air Corps Enlisted Reserve must have reached his seventeenth birthday but not have reached his eighteenth birthday. Written consent of parents for enlistment is required.

An applicant may be single or married.

An applicant must have been a citizen of the United States for at least ten years prior to date of application.

Birth certificate or other properly authenticated proof of date of birth or citizenship must be presented. In the case of an applicant who is a native of one of the Allied Nations and is now a resident of this country, of good reputation and unquestioned loyalty to the United States, a request for waiver of the ten-year citizenship requirement may be submitted to The Adjutant General.

An applicant for voluntary induction or for enlistment in the Air Corps Enlisted Reserve must present, as evidence of his good character, three letters of recommendation from reputable citizens who are not related to him and to whom the applicant is well known.

An enlisted man or the Army of the United States may apply for Aviation Cadet air crew training, provided he has the required qualifications. An enlisted applicant who is found mentally and physically qualified for Aviation Cadet training will be transferred in grade to the Air Corps, unassigned.

Physical. —*General*: An Aviation Cadet candidate must meet the same physical standards as those prescribed for appointment and call to active duty as a Reserve officer in any component of the Army of the United States.

Air Crew. —An Aviation Cadet in training for duty as a flying officer is required to meet special physical standards, somewhat higher than for others. His visual acuity and color perception must be perfectly normal. Hearing must be normal in each ear. A flying officer, except fighter pilot, is required to be not less than 60 nor more than 76 inches in height and to weigh not less than 105 nor more than 200 pounds. A fighter pilot must be not less than 64. nor more than 70 inches in height and must weigh not more than 160 and not less than 114 pounds. Before an Aviation Cadet is eligible to enter upon any flying training, he must pass a complete physical examination for flying duty.

Mental. —*Air Crew*: All candidates for air crew training are required to take a preliminary mental examination which eliminates at the start any who may lack the fundamental knowledge and aptitude necessary to comprehend the instruction given in Army Air Forces schools. This examination is of the multiple-choice, short-answer type. It is designed to give a picture of the general field of knowledge possessed by each candidate but is so wide in scope that any intelligent young man with an average background of study should be able to make a passing grade. No definite amount of formal schooling is required. It does not matter how he gained the knowledge if he can pass the test.

Air Corps Enlisted Reserve. —An applicant for enlistment in the Air Corps Enlisted Reserve must pass an Army mental alertness test to determine his aptitude and suitability for air crew training.

College or Preparatory Pre-Flight Training

Under the College Preparatory Pre-Flight Training Program, Aviation Cadet candidates are enrolled as enlisted men in one of several score colleges and universities throughout the country for a five-month preparatory course, prior to being assigned for flight training in schools of the Flying Training Command.

This course of preparatory instruction is devoted largely to academic subjects. These comprise sixty hours each of English, geography, and modern history; eighty hours of mathematics; and 180 hours of physics. The instruction also comprises twenty-four hours of civil air regulations, 280 hours of basic military indoctrination, including infantry drill, ceremonies and inspections, physical training, interior guard duty, and other military subjects. During this time the Aviation Cadet may also receive ten hours of flight training in cooperation with the Civil Aeronautics Administration.

Air Crew Training

Flying officers are classified as bombardiers, navigators, and pilots, depending upon the type of duty for which they have been trained. The candidate's preference is respected in this matter as far as possible. However, applicants for flying duty training are given further psychological examinations—in addition to the routine screening test—prior to their appointment as Aviation Cadets. The purpose of these tests is to determine the type of training for which each is best suited by aptitude and personal characteristics.

An Aviation Cadet eliminated from air crew training is eligible to apply for ground crew training, provided he meets the basic requirements for such training and is recommended for a particular course. Should he be unable to meet the requirements for ground officer training in the Army Air Forces, he will be relieved as an Aviation Cadet and will revert to an enlisted status. He may then be returned to his former organization in the grade he held at the time of his transfer to the Air Corps, unassigned, or sent in the grade of private to the Air Forces Training Center (Technical).

The Bombardier. —The bombardier's duty, once he becomes a participant in a combat flight, is performed in a matter of seconds—but the most important seconds of the flight. At the crucial moment, when the bomber reaches its objective, the bombardier takes over from the pilot. Upon his skill in landing his bombs on the target depends the success of the entire mission.

The Aviation Cadet who is training to become a bombardier receives twenty-seven weeks instruction. Nine weeks are devoted to fundamentals, six weeks to gunnery and twelve weeks to specialized. Ground training of bombardiers includes the basic theory of bombing, construction and maintenance of bombsights, bombing accessories, bombing procedures, bombing analysis, aircraft observer training, and general military subjects.

Air training of the bombardier includes target identification by day and night, tracking or simulated bombing, and actual bombing practice.

The Navigator. —To the navigator member of an air crew belongs the vital responsibility of plotting the airplane's course to its objective, be it near or far, and or determining at all times the exact position of the craft. He is the man behind the man at the controls, and his instructions enable the pilot to guide the ship directly to its objective.

The training of a navigator requires thirty three weeks. Nine weeks are devoted to study of fundamentals, six weeks to gunnery and eighteen weeks to special navigation subjects.

The navigator receives thorough instruction in the four basic types of navigation: pilotage, calibration, dead reckoning, and celestial.

A stirring poster, created by Jes Wilhelm Schlaikjer in 1944, encourages recruitment to the USAAF with the representation of several aircraft types in formation. (Jes Wilhelm Schlaikjer/USAF)

As for the case of bombardiers, evidence of formal schooling is not required of candidates for training as navigators. However, a definite mathematical bent is essential, and it is desirable that pre-Cadet training should have included a sound fundamental groundwork in mathematics. A knowledge of astronomy will prove useful. Those interested in pursuing their mathematics studies still further, will find an excellent opportunity for doing so in the navigation schools of the U.S. Army Air Forces.

The Pilot. —The pilot is the member of the air crew at the controls, and the flight of the ship on its course is his responsibility. The navigator lays out the course at the end of which is the objective of the flight. It is up to the pilot to get the craft there in the shortest possible time—or at the desired moment, as the case may be. His is the spectacular role. Yet it is gruelling, and his period of training is longer than that of any other member of the air crew.

The Aviation Cadet who is training to become a pilot receives thirty-six weeks' instruction. This instruction is divided into four courses, each of nine weeks' duration. The first course is devoted to fundamentals involving general military training and preliminary groundwork.

Flying training of pilots is divided into three nine-week courses: primary, basic, and advanced, with flying time of sixty to sixty-five, seventy, and eighty hours, respectively. During advanced training the pilot is assigned to bombardment flying or pursuit flying and to twin- or single-engine planes, depending upon his temperament and physique—two important factors in determining the Aviation Cadet's particular field of specialization.

Mechanical aptitude, unusually quick reflexes, perfect physical coordination, and the ability to make rapid decisions are desirable in the applicant who wishes to become a pilot. A knowledge of mathematics and some experience in the field of the applied sciences are useful.

Pay and Special Benefits While Training

Pay of an applicant accepted for Aviation Cadet training through voluntary induction, while undergoing preparatory or pre-flight training, will be that of a private, $50 per month.

Each applicant accepted for air crew training through voluntary induction will sign the following statement which will appear upon his application blank: "I understand that I will be assigned to pre-Aviation Cadet training and will not be appointed an Aviation Cadet until I have completed such training. Further, that should I fail to complete such training, I will be eliminated from the eligible list for Aviation Cadet (air crew) training and be assigned to the Air Corps in the grade of private."

After appointment as an Aviation Cadet, and while in training in that grade, he receives base pay of $75 per month and a ration allowance of $1.00 per day. He is also furnished quarters, medical care, uniforms, and other clothing and equipment. He is given a $10,000 Government Life Insurance policy at Government expense while undergoing actual flying training. After his graduation, and while on flying status, this life insurance policy must be continued at his own expense.

An enlisted man of the Army of the United States, transferred in grade to the Air Corps, unassigned, for Aviation Cadet air crew training, will receive the pay and allowances of his enlisted grade while undergoing the pre-fight training prior to his appointment as an Aviation Cadet.

Pay and Benefits After Completion of Training

An Aviation Cadet who successfully completes the course of air crew training will be commissioned as a second lieutenant or appointed a flight officer in the Army of the United States. He will then be assigned to active duty with the Army Air Forces. He will be given an allowance of $250 for uniforms when he is called to active duty.

Monthly pay and allowances of a second lieutenant or flight officer when on flying duty are as much as $291, if he has no legal dependents. A second lieutenant or flight officer with legal dependents may receive as much as $327 when on flying duty.

The amounts received by a second lieutenant or flight officer, under the conditions described above, include the base pay of his grade, as well as flying pay while on flying status, and allowances for subsistence and quarters. No allowance for quarters will be paid to an officer or flight officer while he his occupying suitable government quarters.

The Long View

Looking beyond the end of the war, it is easy to see that your training in the Army Air Forces will undoubtedly prove of great benefit to you after your return to civil life. Most of us are old enough to remember that commercial aviation as we know it today, came into being following the last war. Largely, it was developed as a result of the lessons learned in that war, and by the men who learned those lessons first-hand. The aviation pioneers of the 'twenties, and aviation kings of the 'thirties, were practically all men who had learned to fly while serving in the Army Air Corps in 1917–1918 and in the years immediately following.

It is not at all unreasonable to predict that following the close of the present war, commercial aviation will develop even more rapidly than it did in the 'twenties. Although it may not be apparent at the moment, things are being learned about planes and methods of flight today that will lift the science of aviation to heretofore undreamed of levels of achievement in the years that are to follow.

Training Mishap

Air training was a risky business, especially during the war years when the sheer volumes of men passing through the system stretched trainers, aircraft, and facilities to the maximum, raising the statistical likelihood of accidents occurring. The following account, told by Captain W. V. Brown in June 1942, shows the perils of primary flight training in the PT-17 Stearman biplane during the 1930s:

I went to Randolph and Kelly Fields ten years ago, as a Flying Cadet. We had a mighty fine class of boys, 208 started I believe, and 83 were graduated. Almost all of the fellows were out of college a year, had worked at depression jobs, and decided that flying held a vastly more impressive future. Besides, Randolph Field had just recently been constructed as a magnificent new training center, and we were all anxious to take a crack at flying at this beautiful field.

We turned out some good men, too. To mention a few: Capt. Bierne Lay, Jr., whose "I Wanted Wings" and other stories have made their mark among the real yarns of flying lore; Jack Strickler, who is designing speedy ships for pursuit pilots; several officers who must remain anonymous who are working night and day to provide better planes by constant testing at Wright Field; scores of crack airline pilots, who are also now ferrying military airplanes for the Allies to all corners of the globe; and the remainder, without exception I believe, occupied with Service flying.

Our training together provided a bond which is closer than any fraternity could ever hope to attain. We lived, slept, talked, ate, drank, and practiced flying as a closely knit unit for one whole year, with the result that we came as close to being 83 brothers with a common purpose as it is possible for unrelated men to be. That is why I like to hear of the present day feats of men from my class, and why I look back fondly on their exploits of the past.

I recall a classmate at Randolph Field who pulled the classic boner of many another unsung pilot. He was making a practice landing during his basic training stage into a comparatively small strange field, when he saw that he was rapidly running out of field while still rolling on the ground at a fast clip. The fence ahead became a prominent landmark on the immediate horizon. An experienced pilot would have opened his throttle and gone around again for another attempt, but not this lad. He figured he could "Whoa, Nellie!" and pull up short; so he practically stood on his brakes and promptly flipped over on his back.

He was flying a biplane trainer, comparatively large and sturdy, and when the dust cleared and he had oriented himself, he could see that his ship was resting comfortably on its upper wing with the fuselage well above and parallel to the ground, he himself gazing back down the field upon which he had just tried to land, with his normal vision somewhat distorted, since he was hanging upside down in his seat, with only his tautly stretched safety belt accomplishing his defiance of gravity.

Thoughtfully considering the safety of his airplane and mindful of the fire hazard, as he hung slothlike in his cockpit, he carefully cut off his ignition and all other electrical switches, closed his fuel selector valve, and after deciding that he was unhurt and ready to leave the ship in good order, he released his safety belt with a flip of the catch and immediately fell on his head to the ground four feet below, knocking himself out and spraining his neck to such an extent that his recovery required a three weeks tour in the hospital.

CHAPTER 2

Pilot and Copilot

Although any air crew role had a certain cachet, the position of pilot had the lion's share of public glamor attached to it, thus many potential recruits aspired to join the USAAF in a bomber's cockpit. Yet few made the grade. Piloting a bomber aircraft required a supreme package of capabilities—the core activity of flying an aircraft was just the tip of a very large technical iceberg. The pilot would have to master advanced mechanical and electrical engineering, airframe and powerplant design, armament systems, navigational tools and methods, meteorology, radio communications, bomb aiming, combat formation flying, enemy aircraft and flak capabilities, first aid, and much more. As the first manual extract below demonstrates, however, all the technical knowledge in the world didn't matter if the pilot and copilot did not exhibit exceptional leadership qualities. The entire crew of the bomber, often operating under desperate fear and stress, would look to their commander for fast, authoritative judgements and a calm demeanor that projected a sense of control, even if the pilot, usually only a few years older than the rest of the crew, was fighting his own terror internally.

Pilot Training for the B-24 Liberator *was published on May 1, 1945. The date of the manual is significant—the German surrender in Europe would come the following day, although fighting in Asia and the Pacific continued until September. The manual therefore incorporates the full breadth of combat flying experience gained in the European Theater of Operations (ETO). Of note below are the general points made about bomber crew responsibilities, but we also see some of the fundamental principles of formation bombing, the core tactic applied to the area bombing of targets in Germany, occupied Europe and other Axis nations. The missions varied between "milk runs" of a few hours over accessible*

819 B.S. - 1·23·4 5 - 01538 - LT. KNUDSON

Ground and flying crew gather in front of the nose of the B-24 Liberator *The Liberty Bell*, which operated with the 819th Bombardment Squadron, 30th Bomb Group. (USAAF)

and lightly protected targets to numbing 10-hour ordeals out to Berlin and back. Throughout, the pilot and copilot had to be steady hands.

From *Pilot Training Manual for the B-24 Liberator* (1945)

Duties and responsibilities of the Airplane Commander

Here's where they separate the men from the boys. You can be one of the best B-24 pilots ever trained and still fail as an airplane commander. In addition to qualifying yourself as a top–flight pilot, you have the job of building a fighting team that you can rely on in any emergency. Failure of any member of the crew to do the right thing at the right time may mean failure of your mission, unnecessary loss of life and possible loss of your airplane.

You Can't Pass the Buck

Your authority as airplane commander carries with it responsibility that you cannot shirk. Your engineer is a trained specialist, but his training is incomplete. He knows how to transfer fuel, but does he know how to transfer it in the particular airplane you are flying? It isn't enough that he thinks so. You must know what he knows. It is up to you to perfect the basic training he has been given. An oversight of this kind cost a B-24 and 2 lives in the Pacific. You are now flying a 10-man weapon. It is your airplane, and your crew. You are responsible for the safety and efficiency of the crew at all times—not just when you are flying, but for the full 24 hours of every day while you are in command.

Your crew is made up of specialists. Each man—whether he is the navigator, bombardier, engineer, radio operator, or one of the gunners—is an expert in his line. But how well he does his job, and how efficiently he plays his part as a member of your combat team, will depend to a great extent on how well you play your own part as the airplane commander.

Know Your Crew

Learn all you can about each member of your crew just as soon after he joins your outfit as possible. Where is his home? What is his education? Is he married? What jobs has he had? Where did he get his flight training? How does he like the idea of being assigned to a B-24?

Your job is to learn all you can about each crew member so you can evaluate his qualifications, initiative, proficiency and reliability.

Know His Personal Habits

It is no business of yours whether a crew member spends his free hours in prayer, gambling, or hunting turtle's eggs unless these habits interfere with the proper performance of his duty. Then his business is your business. You can't afford to see a mission jeopardized because a crew member doesn't get enough sleep, comes to duty with a hangover, starts on a high-altitude mission with gas-producing food in his stomach, or is so distracted by worry that he cannot concentrate on the task at hand.

See that your men are properly quartered, clothed, and fed. There will be many times, when your airplane and crew are away from the home base, when you may even have to carry your interest to the extent of financing them yourself. Remember always that you are the commanding officer of a miniature army—a specialized army; and that morale is one of the biggest problems for the commander of any, army, large or small.

Crew Discipline

Your success as the airplane commander will depend in a large measure on the respect, confidence, and trust which the crew feels for you. It will depend also on how well you maintain crew discipline.

Your position commands obedience and respect. This does not mean that you have to be stiff-necked, overbearing, or aloof. Such characteristics certainly will defeat your purpose.

Be friendly, understanding, but firm. Know your job, and, by the way you perform your duties daily, impress upon the crew that you do know your job. Keep close to your men and let them realize that their interests are uppermost in your mind. Make fair decisions, after due consideration of all the facts involved; but make them in such a way as to impress upon your crew that your decisions are made to stick.

Crew discipline is vitally important, but it need not be as difficult a problem as it sounds. Good discipline in an air crew breeds comradeship and high morale. And the combination is unbeatable.

You can be a good CO and still be a regular guy. You can command respect from your men, and still be one of them.

"To associate discipline with informality, comradeship, a levelling of rank, and at times a shift in actual command away from the leader, may seem paradoxical," says a former combat group commander. "Certainly, it isn't down the military groove. But it is discipline just the same—and the kind of discipline that brings success in the air."

Crew Training

Train your crew as a team. Keep abreast of their training. It won't be possible for you to follow each man's courses of instruction, but you can keep a close check on his record and progress.

Get to know each man's duties and problems. Know his job and try to devise ways and means of helping him to perform it more efficiently.

Each crew member naturally feels great pride in the importance of his particular specialty. You can help him to develop this pride to include the manner in which he performs that duty. To do that you must possess and maintain a very thorough knowledge of each man's job and the problems he has to deal with in the performance of his duties.

Are You Ready to Fight?

Are your guns working? The only way you can be sure is to know how competent and reliable your gunners are. It is uncomfortable to get caught by a swarm of enemy fighters and find that your guns won't function.

What about your navigator? You can't do his job for him throughout training in the states and expect him to guide you safely over a thousand miles of water to a speck on the map. Remember that there aren't any check points in the ocean and you have to rely on your navigator.

Your bombs miss the target. Long hours of flying wasted ... why? It may be because the bombsight gyro was not turned on long enough in advance or because the bombsight was not kept warm by means of the heater so that when the bombardier put his warm face to the eyepiece, it fogged up and was unusable. Who is at fault? The bombardier is, of course, primarily to blame, but in the background, there is usually lack of leadership, guidance and inspiration. No crew is ever any more on the ball than its airplane commander.

Practical Questions

1. Are you the airplane commander, qualifying yourself to do justice to your crew?
2. Can all of your crew fly at high altitudes without discomfort or physical handicap?
3. Does anyone in your crew get airsick?
4. Are the turret gunners too big for their turrets?
5. Can the copilot take over in emergency?
6. Does the radio operator understand DF [direction finding] aids?
7. Do the gunners know how to unload and stow their guns?
8. Do the engineer and the copilot (and do you) know how to use the load adjuster and how to load the airplane properly?

9. Do the engineer and copilot (and you) use the control charts on every flight to check your knowledge of power settings and the efficient performance of your airplane?
10. Does your crew know emergency procedures and signals?
11. Is each member of your crew properly equipped?
12. What can you do to prevent or relieve anoxia, air sickness, fatigue?
13. Who is qualified to render first aid?
14. How's the morale of your outfit? Are they eager or do they sluff off?
15. How will your crew react in emergency?
   These are just a few of the practical questions you as airplane commander must be able to answer to your own satisfaction.

RULES TO BE ENFORCED ON EVERY FLIGHT BY THE AIRPLANE COMMANDER

1. Smoking

   a. No smoking in airplane at an altitude of less than 1000 feet.
   b. No smoking during fuel transfer.
   c. Never carry lighted cigarette through bomb bays.
   d. Never attempt to throw a lighted cigarette from the airplane. Put it out first.

2. Parachutes

   a. All persons aboard will wear parachute harness at all times from takeoff to landing.
   b. Each person aboard will have a parachute on every flight.

3. Propellers

   a. No person will walk through propellers at any time whether they are turning or not.
   b. No person will leave the airplane when propellers are turning unless personally ordered to do so by the airplane commander.

4. Oxygen Masks

a. Oxygen masks will be carried on all day flights where altitude may exceed 10,000 feet and on all night flights, regardless of altitude.

b. Day: All persons will use oxygen starting at 7,000 to 10,000 feet on all day flights where altitude at any time will exceed 10,000 feet.

c. Night: All persons will use oxygen from the ground up on all flights during which altitude may exceed 10,000 feet.

5. Training

a. Tell your crew the purpose of each mission and what you expect each to accomplish.

b. Keep the crew busy throughout the flight. Get position reports from the navigator; send them out through the radio operator. Put the engineer to work in the cruise control and maximum range charts. Require the copilot to keep a record of engine performance. Give them a workout. Encourage them to use their skill. Let them sleep in their own bunks—not in a B-24. A team is an active outfit. Make the most of every practice mission.

c. Practice all emergency procedures at least once a week; bailout, ditching and fire drill.

6. Inspections

a. Check your airplane with reference to the particular mission you are undertaking. Check everything.

b. Check your crew for equipment, preparedness and understanding.

7. Interphone

a. Keep the interphone chattering. Ask for immediate reports of aircraft, trains, and ships just as you would expect them in combat—with proper identification.

b. Require interphone reports every 15 minutes from all crew men when on oxygen.

The cockpit of the B-17G Flying Fortress *Sentimental Journey*, which entered service in 1944 but remains airworthy to this day. (Darren Kirby CC BY-SA 2.0)

SUGGESTED COMBAT CREW DUTY ASSIGNMENTS

PILOT
>Principal duty: Airplane Commander
>Secondary duty: Pilot
>Added duty: Navigation Specialist

COPILOT
>Principal duty: Assistant Airplane Commander
>Secondary duty: Airplane Engineering Officer and Assistant Pilot
>Added duty: Fire Officer
>Added duty: Navigational Specialist
>Added duty: Gunfire Control Officer

NAVIGATOR
>Principal duty: Navigator
>Secondary duty: Qualified as Nose Turret Gunner
>Added duty: Assistant Bombardier

Added duty: Oxygen and Equipment Officer
Added duty: First Aid Specialist

BOMBARDIER
Principal duty: Bombardier
Secondary duty: Qualified as Nose Turret Gunner
Added duty: Airplane Armament Officer
Added duty: Navigation Specialist

AERIAL ENGINEER
Principal duty: Aerial Engineer
Secondary duty: Top Turret Gunner
Added duty: Qualified for Copilot Duties
Added duty: Parachute Officer
Added duty: First Aid Specialist
Added duty: Assistant Radio Operator

RADIO OPERATOR
Principal duty: Radio Operator
Secondary duty: Waist Gunner
Added duty: Assistant Airplane Engineer
Added duty: First Aid Specialist
Added duty: Qualified as Top Turret Gunner

NOSE TURRET GUNNER
Principal duty: Nose Turret Gunner
Secondary duty: Turret Specialist
Added duty: Assistant to Armament Officer

BELLY TURRET GUNNER
Principal duty: Belly Turret Gunner
Secondary duty: Turret Specialist

TAIL TURRET GUNNER
Principal duty: Tail Turret Gunner
Secondary duty: Turret Specialist
Added duty: Assistant to Parachute Officer

Purpose of Assigning Added Duties

These assignments are not just so many titles. Each duty represents a specific job to be done. As airplane commander, you are responsible for everything but you can't do everything.

These assignments, properly explained, will arouse the enthusiasm, energy and initiative of your crew. You have the right to demand that each crew member become an expert and maintain expert status in the particular duties assigned to him. There is nothing ironclad about the added duty assignments. These can be shifted around if there is a clear-cut advantage in doing so. For example, the suggested added duty of the crew oxygen and equipment officer can be shifted from the navigator to the bombardier or to one of the other crew members if he is better qualified or indicates a greater interest in the problem. The main thing is to spread the duties, encourage the individual to become an expert and then require him to educate and supervise the rest of the crew regarding his particular specialty. Ask the crew member to read all he can and learn all he can about his specific duties; to be prepared to conduct and aid in inspections and drills, and to give the crew periodic instruction in his specialty. You, as airplane commander, are the sparkplug of this plan. You will assign duties, call drills, and give your specialists as much opportunity as possible to spread their knowledge.

To aid you, here are definitions of some of the less understood added duties.

Definitions of Added Duties

Airplane Engineering Officer—It is the duty of this officer (almost always the copilot) to know more about the airplane than any member of the crew and to see that all other crew members are instructed in all procedures pertaining to the airplane. The engineering officer should be able, by judicious questioning, to size up a new flight engineer in a few minutes' time. He should be able to perform any of the flight engineer's duties. It is his job to see that all crew members are instructed in the proper methods of transferring fuel. He is charged with the duty of seeing that proper records of engine operations are kept from flight to flight so that faulty operation will be detected before it becomes serious. He should be intimately familiar with the cruise control, climb, and maximum range charts and should educate the engineer in their use.

Gunfire Control Officer—It has been found that the copilot is in the best position to serve as gunfire control officer. He has the best view of developing attacks, although he cannot possibly see all enemy fighters. Although he does not attempt to actively direct the fire from all guns, he does supervise the calling of attacks, maintains strict interphone discipline, and sees that the plan and procedure for controlling fire is strictly followed. He is responsible for seeing that the crew is properly indoctrinated in the use of the throat microphone and established practice-mission procedures which will simulate as nearly as possible the interphone conversations that would be necessary in combat. In the heat of battle, crew members tend to talk too fast, speak in too high a tone, or allow the microphone to be improperly placed. The gunfire control officer will develop the interphone proficiency to a point where absolute cooperation between gun stations can be maintained on interphone.

Navigation Specialist—Individuals with this assignment should understand all aids to navigation, understand how the navigator's log is kept, and be able in emergency to ascertain the location of the airplane and help to bring it back to base. Obviously, these men cannot be fully qualified navigators, but should know everything possible about navigation procedures that may be of aid in case the navigator is incapacitated.

Oxygen and Equipment Officer—This job requires a detailed understanding of the equipment and its operation. This officer confers with the personal equipment officer of the squadron regarding the use of all equipment, precautions to be taken, proper fit and care, and sees that all crew members are properly instructed. He makes periodic inspections of the crew as directed by the pilot to see that oxygen equipment is properly fitted and used. He checks all crew members on the use of walk-around bottles and sees that correct procedures are followed on high-altitude missions.

First-Aid Specialist—This assignment should be given, as far as possible, to individuals who already have a good knowledge of first aid. However, there should be one specialist in the nose, one in the rear compartment and one on the flight deck. If individuals in these compartments are not familiar with first aid, pilot should see that they receive adequate instruction. Combat reports reveal that lack of knowledge of first aid has cost lives on combat missions.

Fire Officer—This officer, usually the copilot, should know the location of all fire-fighting apparatus and know specifically when and how to use it. He should instruct the entire crew on their exact duties in case of fires. He will arrange a program of fire drill with the pilot, aid in conducting the drill, and point out all mistakes. He will conduct a periodic inspection of the ship for fire hazards, see that the fire prevention rules are obeyed and be responsible to the pilot for proper precautions against fire.

Qualified as Turret Gunner—Crew members whose stations are adjacent to turrets should be able to take over the turret and operate it if emergency requires. Turret specialists instruct such crew members in the operation of the turret and use spare time in flight and on the ground to qualify such crew members as emergency turret gunners. Then they can give assistance in case of trouble with the turret or if the turret specialist is incapacitated.

Airplane Armament Officer—The armament officer must be familiar with all armament the airplane carries, the protection it provides and how it can best be used. In addition to his duties in connection with the loading, arming and dropping of bombs, he aids the pilot in enforcing the safety regulations regarding practice bombing, practice gunnery, and proper loading, unloading, and stowing of guns. In case of accidental discharge of a gun, he, with the gunner and pilot, will usually be considered at fault, on the ground that he has insufficiently instructed the gunner in procedures and precautions.

Parachute Officer—This officer will see that each crew member has his own properly fitted parachute, that he knows how to use it, that he knows how and where to leave the plane and how to open the chute and descend. He will plan a drill schedule with the pilot and aid in parachute drill. Through the pilot he will see that rules regarding the care, inspection, fitting and wearing of parachutes are observed in accordance with AAF regulations and requirements.

Turret Specialist—The turret specialist must know not only how to operate his turret but how to repair it and put it back in operation if necessary. He will give instruction at every opportunity to crew members near his station to qualify them as assistant turret gunners.

Assistant Assignments—An assistant is one who can take over a job and do it as well as the regularly assigned individual if necessary. The assistant radio operator, for example, should be able to take over and operate the radio as well (or almost as well) as the regular radio operator, etc. The most valuable man on a team is the one who can take over other jobs than his own if and when required to do so. The above is by no means a complete statement of this problem but it should give the airplane commander the idea of what it means to "train your crew," for every man to "know every other man's job," and what is meant by teamwork. These are not empty phrases. Every 15 minutes wasted on a mission means your crew is 15 minutes less well prepared for combat. There is no reason for your radio equipment to be idle. Your engineer has no time to sleep or sit and vegetate if he is carrying out his job of teaching all crew members to transfer fuel, working the cruise control charts, really keeping on the ball. You have to fly a practice mission ... so why not run it so that your crew will get all they can out of it? It is real pleasure to develop top-notch proficiency and teamwork, and your crew will actually enjoy missions more if they feel that their skills are being utilized to the fullest extent, if only in practice. It is worth while to discuss here also the principal duties of each of the crew members to aid the commander in judging their ability.

COPILOT

The copilot is the executive officer: your chief assistant, understudy, and strong right arm. He must be familiar enough with every one of your duties—both as pilot and airplane commander—and be able to take over and act in your place at any time.

He must be able to fly the airplane under all conditions as well as you would fly it yourself.

He must be extremely proficient in engine operation and know instinctively what to do to keep the airplane flying smoothly even though he is not handling the controls.

He must have a thorough knowledge of cruising control data and know how to apply it at the proper time.

He is also the engineering officer aboard the airplane and maintains a complete log of performance data.

He must be a qualified instrument pilot.

He must be qualified to navigate during day or night by pilotage, dead reckoning, and by use of radio aids.

He must be proficient in the operation of all radio equipment located in the pilot's compartment. In formation flying, he must be able to make engine adjustments almost automatically.

He must be prepared to take over on instruments when the formation is climbing through an overcast, thus enabling you to watch the rest of the formation.

Always remember that the copilot is a fully trained, rated pilot just like yourself. He is subordinate to you only by virtue of your position as the airplane commander. But the B-24 is a lot of airplane; more airplane than any one pilot can handle alone over a long period of time. Therefore, you have been provided with a second pilot who will share the duties of flight operation.

Treat your copilot as a brother pilot. Remember that the more proficient he is as a pilot, the more efficiently he will be able to perform the duties of the vital post he holds as your second in command.

Be sure that he is always allowed to do his share of the flying, in the copilot's seat, on takeoffs, landings, and on instruments.

The importance of the copilot is eloquently testified by airplane commanders overseas. There have been numerous cases in which the pilot has been disabled or killed in flight and the copilot has taken full command of both airplane and crew, completed the mission, and. returned safely to the home base. Usually, the copilots who have distinguished themselves under such conditions have been copilots who have been respected and trained by the airplane commander as pilots.

Bear in mind that the pilot in the right-hand seat of your airplane is preparing himself for an airplane commander's post too. Allow him every chance to develop his ability and to profit by your experience.

[. . .]

TAKEOFF

Takeoffs are easy and smooth in the B-24 provided there is plenty of room and you use proper technique. Tricycle gear improves both the takeoff and landing characteristics. Be sure before you leave the line that the runway is long enough (considering altitude, temperature, etc.) and be sure there are no obstructions in your line of flight.

Taxiing Into Position

Get your clearance from the tower to line up on the runway. Take a good look for aircraft and taxi out in a wide sweep using a minimum of runway for straightening the nosewheel. Stop the airplane lined up straight ahead, hold your position with the brakes, and set all throttles at 1,000 rpm. Both pilot and copilot should make a final quick check on all instruments. Then copilot obtains a radio clearance for take-off and you are ready for the take-off run.

The Takeoff Run

1. Release the brakes and slowly but steadily advance all throttles together. Learn to apply power at the speed engines can readily take it. Never jam or stiff-arm the throttles.

2. If you start to move to the left of the middle of the runway lead the throttles on the left, and vice versa. Don't stop the opposite set of throttles, but instead lead all throttles progressively. In this manner you can build up speed rapidly and obtain rudder control quickly. **Don't ever** attempt to control direction on take-off by the use of brakes.

3. As soon as you have rudder control, use it! Come in with lots of rudder to hold your line down the runway, rather than using excessive and unnecessary build-up of power on one side.

4. Copilot follows throttles through with his left hand, and as soon as they are against the stops, he sets the friction lock to prevent throttles from creeping but so they still can be easily moved. **Note:** Pilot's hand should be on the throttles throughout the takeoff except when necessary to trim the plane or signal the copilot. Whenever pilot's hand leaves the throttles, copilot should hold them. Copilot should closely observe all instruments (particularly manifold pressure and rpm). Use full throttle on takeoff. This shortens the run and minimizes wear and tear on tires and gear. Manifold pressure

should not exceed 49" for Grade 100 fuel or 42.7" for Grade 91 fuel and propellers should not exceed 2,700 rpm. Power reduction necessary to keep within manifold pressure limits should be made with the throttles and not with the turbo regulators.

5. As your speed increases to 70 or 80 mph so that you have elevator control, ease back on the control column just enough to relieve the nose-wheel of its weight. When full weight is on the nosewheel, the wing is at a negative angle of attack; lifting the weight puts the wing in the desired slightly positive angle.

6. Hold this attitude straight down the runway, and the airplane will fly itself off the ground at 120 to 130 mph, depending on the gross weight. Don't haul it off, however, and be sure the attitude is correct. If you apply too much back pressure, pulling the nose too far up, you establish too great an angle of attack, which creates more lift and puts the plane into the air at a lower airspeed—110 mph, for example. Then, if you lower the nose to pick up airspeed, you decrease the angle of attack and therefore decrease the lift. The airplane cannot accelerate fast enough to compensate for this changed angle, and the result will be that you settle back on the ground. So don't try to make the airplane fly—let it fly itself. Once it does, increase the back pressure just enough to establish a shallow positive climb, and **hold it**.

Note: Even if you have to get the airplane into the air at a low airspeed (in a short-field take-off, for instance), don't lower the nose; hold your angle of attack and let the airspeed build up gradually.

7. Don't become over-anxious about building up climbing speed. It takes time for the power of the propeller thrust to overcome the inertia of a heavy airplane. Beware of lowering the nose below level flight to build up airspeed. Always make all changes of attitude gradually, a little at a time. Make frequent small changes rather than large ones. As your airspeed increases, relieve heavy fore or aft control pressure by trimming.

If you set artificial horizon properly before take-off, with the miniature airplane slightly below the horizon bar, you can hold the proper angle of climb after leaving the runway by keeping the miniature airplane approximately ⅛-inch above the horizon bar. Establish and hold proper attitudes in the B-24 by reference to flight instruments rather than to outside objects. It's an instrument plane.

8. Attain a minimum airspeed of 140 mph and a safe altitude above all objects before your first power reduction.

AFTER-TAKEOFF CHECK
Amplified Checklist

1. **Wheels**. Copilot raises gear on signal from the pilot, (usually thumb jerked upward). As soon as the gear handle is in the "UP" position, pilot stops the wheels with smooth, firm application of brakes. This reduces the strain on the main gear suspension assemblies caused by the gyroscopic action of rapidly rotating wheels. Rough application of brakes puts undue strain on the gear fittings and may rupture an expander tube.

Important
The copilot reads the after-takeoff checklist when the gear and flaps are up, the first power reduction is completed, and when a safe altitude and an airspeed of 150 mph are reached.

Caution: There is no hurry about raising the wheels. Be sure you have plenty of airspeed and altitude before you start them up.

When the copilot raises the gear, he should be sure to press down the safety button located on top of the gear handle to unlock it. Forcing the handle against the lock will injure the locking pin.

If the solenoid latch does not release, you can push the releasing pin in with a screwdriver and then raise the gear handle to bring the wheels up. The latch is located behind the pilot's instrument panel just forward

B-24 Liberators of the 404th Bomb Squadron taxi out in freezing conditions on the airfield at Shemya, Alaska in early 1945. (USGOV-PD)

of the pedestal. **Don't try this on the ground because you will retract the gear and the airplane will crash down on its belly**.

2. **Superchargers**. When the airplane attains safe airspeed (140 mph) and altitude, the pilot makes the first power reduction with superchargers and sets them for normal climb (not to exceed 46″ for Grade 100 or 38″ for Grade 91 fuels).
   Power Reduction with Electronic Turbo Control: Turn the turbo control dial back toward zero until you reach the desired manifold pressure.

3. **Throttles**. If manifold pressure remains higher than desired for climb after superchargers are all the way off, then retard the throttle to obtain climbing manifold pressure.

4. **Propellers**. Copilot reduces rpm to 2,550 when requested by the pilot.

5. **Wing Flaps**. Copilot raises them when directed by the pilot. Don't raise the flaps before you have altitude of 500 feet and an

airspeed of 140 mph. Remember that changes in flaps change the lift effect of the wing. As you raise the flaps, raise the nose of the airplane to correct for change in attitude. Use enough back pressure to maintain altitude and the airplane will rapidly accelerate to 150 mph. Don't lower the nose to gain this speed because this will result in unnecessary loss of altitude. Add nose-up elevator trim to help maintain your altitude. In heavily loaded aircraft, it is advisable to raise the flaps from 20° to full up in two or three stages. **Warning:** Don't be in a hurry. Get a safe airspeed and a safe altitude before you raise the flaps. But don't let airspeed exceed 155 mph with flaps down.

6. **Booster Pumps**. Copilot switches them off one at a time above 1,000 feet and notes any drop in pressure.

7. **Cowl Flaps**. Will normally be at trail for the climb, checked and set by the copilot.

[. . .]

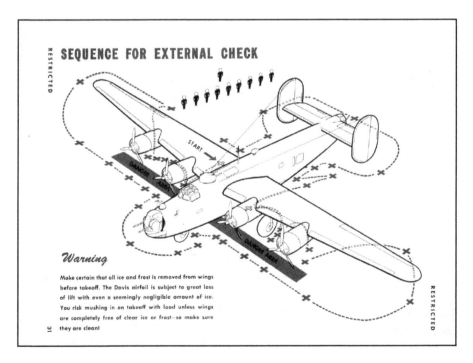

SEQUENCE FOR EXTERNAL CHECK

RESTRICTED

START

DANGER AREA

Warning

Make certain that all ice and frost is removed from wings before takeoff. The Davis airfoil is subject to great loss of lift with even a seemingly negligible amount of ice. You risk mushing in on takeoff with load unless wings are completely free of clear ice or frost—so make sure they are clean!

FORMATION FLYING

When you get into combat you will learn that your best assurance of becoming a veteran of World War II is the good, well-planned, and well-executed formation.

Formation flying is the first requisite of successful operation of heavy bombers in combat. Groups that are noted for their proficiency in formation flying are usually the groups with the lowest casualty rates. Proper formation provides controlled and concentrated firepower, maneuverability, cross-cover, and precise bombing pattern, and permits most effective fighter protection.

Heavy Bomber Formations

Formation flying in 4-engine aircraft presents greater problems than in smaller aircraft. The problems increase in almost direct proportion to the airplane's size and weight. In the B-24, relatively slower response to power and control changes requires a much higher degree of anticipation on the part of the pilot. Therefore, you must allow a greater factor of safety.

Violent maneuvers are dangerous and the necessity for them is seldom encountered. Close flying becomes an added hazard; it accomplishes no purpose and is not even an indication of a good formation. Remember that it is much more difficult to maintain position when flying with proper spacing than with wings overlapping.

"Safety first" is a prerequisite of a good heavy bomber formation because of the number of lives and amount of equipment for which the pilot is responsible.

Clearance in Training Formations

When flying the Vee formation in training, aircraft must not be flown closer to one another than one-half airplane span from nose to tail, and one-half airplane span from wingtip to wingtip. These minimum distances are to be maintained under all formation flying conditions. Keep yourself posted on current AAF regulations concerning clearances in formation flying, since they may change.

Taxiing Out

After engines have been started, all planes stand by on proper frequency. The squadron formation leader checks with the planes in his formation, then calls the tower and clears his formation for taxi and takeoff instructions. As he taxies out, No. 2 man follows, then No. 3, etc., each airplane taking the respective place on the ground that is assigned to it in the air. As soon as the leader parks at an angle near the end of the takeoff strip, the other aircraft do the same. At this point all planes run up engines and prepare for takeoff. The leader makes certain that everyone is ready to go before he pulls onto the takeoff strip.

Takeoff

Squadron formation takeoffs should be cleared from the airdrome in a rapid and efficient manner. Individual takeoffs will be made, and the following procedure is suggested.

The leader goes into takeoff position and takes off at H hour. No. 2 man starts pulling into position as soon as the leader begins to roll. When the leader's wheels leave the runway, No. 2 starts taking off, thus creating a time lapse of about 30 seconds between takeoffs. Similarly, No. 3 follows No. 2, etc. The leader flies straight ahead at 150 mph, 300–500 feet per minute ascent, for one minute plus 30 seconds for each airplane in the formation. He levels off at 1000 feet in order to avoid necessitating high rates of climb for succeeding planes, and cruises at 150 mph.

As soon as the leader has flown out the exact required time, he makes a 180° half-needle-width turn to the left. The second airplane in formation assumes the outside, or No. 2, position, while the third airplane assumes the inside, or No. 3, position. The leader of the second element assumes position on the outside of the formation and the airplanes in his formation assemble on him in the same manner.

3-Airplane Vee

The 3-airplane Vee is the standard formation and the basic one from which other formations are developed. Variations of the Vee offer a concentration of firepower for defense under close control with sufficient

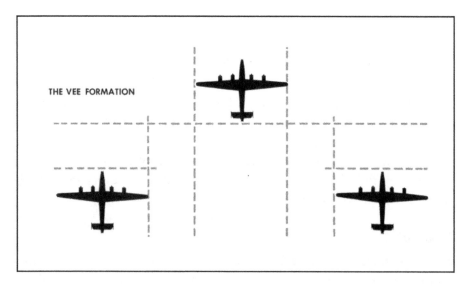

THE VEE FORMATION

maneuverability for all normal missions and afford a bombing pattern which is most effective.

Flight of 6

A formation of 6 aircraft is known as a squadron and is composed of two 3-airplane Vees. At least 50 feet vertical clearance must be maintained between elements in a squadron, with a minimum horizontal clearance of half an airplane's length between the leader of the second element and the wingmen of the first element.

From the basic squadron formation of 6 aircraft the group, made up of 12 to 18 aircraft, is formed. With but small variations, this can be changed to the combat formations used overseas. It is the purpose of training to teach a basic formation which can be readily understood and flown by students and easily adapted to tactical use.

Spacing of Wing Positions

It is particularly important for the leader to avoid violent maneuvers or improper positions which will cause undue difficulty for the wingmen.

The spacing of the wing positions in Vee formation is:

1. Vertically: On the level of the lead airplane.

2. Laterally: Far enough to the side to insure one-half airplane span clearance between the wingtips of the lead airplane and the wing airplane.
3. Longitudinally: Far enough to the rear to insure one-half airplane length clearance between the tail of the lead airplane and the nose of the wing airplane.

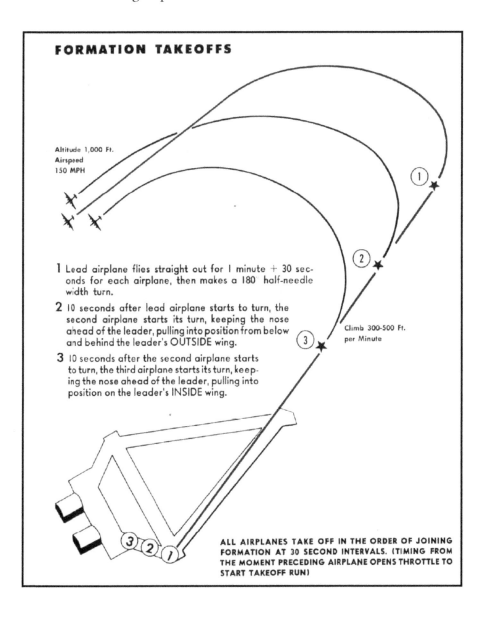

FORMATION TAKEOFFS

Altitude 1,000 Ft.
Airspeed
150 MPH

1 Lead airplane flies straight out for 1 minute + 30 seconds for each airplane, then makes a 180° half-needle width turn.

2 10 seconds after lead airplane starts to turn, the second airplane starts its turn, keeping the nose ahead of the leader, pulling into position from below and behind the leader's OUTSIDE wing.

3 10 seconds after the second airplane starts to turn, the third airplane starts its turn, keeping the nose ahead of the leader, pulling into position on the leader's INSIDE wing.

Climb 300-500 Ft. per Minute

ALL AIRPLANES TAKE OFF IN THE ORDER OF JOINING FORMATION AT 30 SECOND INTERVALS. (TIMING FROM THE MOMENT PRECEDING AIRPLANE OPENS THROTTLE TO START TAKEOFF RUN)

Turns in Vee formation should maintain the relative position of all airplanes in the element.

Practice Trail Formations

A formation is in trail when all airplanes are in the same line and slightly below the airplane ahead. The distance between airplanes will be such that the nose of each airplane is slightly to the rear of the tail of the airplane ahead. It is important that this distance be properly maintained, since if it becomes too great the propeller wash of the airplane ahead will cause difficulty in maintaining formation. Trail formations are to be used only when there are from 3 to 6 aircraft involved, and for purposes of changing the lead, changing wingmen, training in leading elements, and as an optional approach to peel-off for landing.

Changing Wing Position in Training

When changing from Vee to Trail, the wingman into whom a turn is made while in Vee assumes the No. 2 position in Trail, while the outside man takes No. 3 position. When return from Trail to Vee, the No. 3 man in Trail assumes the inside position of the Vee. Remember this, for it is the procedure for changing from Vee to Trail and from Trail to Vee. Also, as explained below, it provides a method for changing positions in a Vee formation.

It is often desirable for a leader to change the wing positions of his formation, i.e., to reverse the right and left positions. This maneuver offers danger of collision unless it is executed properly in accordance with a prearranged plan. A safe procedure is for the leader to announce on the radio that the formation will go into Trail on his first turn. If the turn is executed to the right, it results in the inside man, or No. 2 wingman, becoming No. 2 in the Trail, and the outside man, or No. 3 wingman, being No. 3 in the Trail when the turn is completed. The leader then announces that the formation will re-form in Vee when the Trail executes a turn to the right. This second turn to the right re-forms the Vee with the wingmen reversed.

As stated previously, this results in the No. 2 man of the Trail assuming the outside position of the Vee, as the No. 3 man takes the inside position.

Before making each turn it is desirable for the leader to designate the ultimate position that each wing man is to assume. This will insure complete understanding of the maneuver.

Changing Lead in Training

The formation goes into Trail from the usual 90° turn to the right or left. The leader of the formation makes a 45° turn to the left and flies that heading for approximately 20 seconds or until a turn back will place him in the rear of the formation. When the No. 1 airplane starts his 45° turn, the No. 2 plane in the Trail immediately becomes the leader of the formation and continues to fly straight ahead. At the end of 20 seconds or thereabouts, the original leader turns back and takes up the No. 3 position in his element, or the No. 6 position if in a flight of 6, and notifies the new leader that the maneuver is complete.

Landing from Vee of Squadron in Training

The formation approaches the airdrome at traffic pattern altitude, into the wind up the landing runway, at which time the wheels are ordered down by the leader and the checklist accomplished. Flaps are lowered 20° and an air speed of 135–140 mph established. The leader signals No. 3, when over the edge of the landing runway, to peel off, No. 3 acknowledging by peeling off. No. 1 follows, No. 2 following No. 1, No. 6 following No. 2 and so on.

If there is more than one squadron in the formation, the second makes a 360° turn above traffic pattern altitude and approaches the field after the first squadron has completed its peel-off. Peel-off does not mean a chandelle or a dive. It should consist of a moderate, level turn until the airplane is definitely away from the rest of the formation.

Conclusion

This fact cannot be too strongly stated: a good formation is a safe formation. Air collisions usually result from carelessness or lack of clear understanding between members of the formation. If the simple rules given here are followed explicitly there should be no excuse for mistakes in the air. A mistake in formation flying may mean a costly, irreparable loss of lives and equipment.

Senior pilots of 407th Bomb Squadron, 92nd Bomb Group, line up in front of the B-17F *Flag Ship* at Alconbury Airfield, England. This aircraft was lost in action on November 16, 1943. (USAAF)

Remember that flying too close is not a display of skill; it is a display of bad judgment and lack of common sense.

Tips on Formation Flying

1. Set rpm to minimum allowable for the maximum manifold pressure you expect to use.
2. At altitudes where superchargers are needed, set superchargers to give about 5" more manifold pressure than the average being used.
3. Use throttles to increase and decrease power in maintaining position. Very small corrections should suffice, if you think ahead of the airplane and anticipate necessary changes, and if you give the correction time to take hold. But when far out of position, or when catching up with a formation, increase rpm to maintain proper manifold pressure and rpm relationships.
4. When under attack, use all available power required to stay in formation.
5. In order to keep formation when operating on three engines it is necessary for pilot and copilot to react as a team in applying the required new power settings while the airplane still has momentum

and before it falls behind. If you wait too long before increasing power you drop back out of formation and have a difficult time catching up.

6. When changing leads in practice formations or in Trail positions, avoid closing to proper formation position too rapidly. This can be dangerous.

7. In moving about in position, move the airplane in a direction that will not interfere with or endanger any other aircraft in the formation. In route formation, aircraft should be spread in width rather than depth, thereby being able to resume tight formation quickly.

8. Remember that at high altitudes the rate of closure is much more rapid than at low altitudes; you may have difficulty in slowing down quickly enough. Therefore, you have to begin stopping the closure much sooner. On the other hand, acceleration is slower, so that your anticipation of change in position must be more acute.

B-17Gs of the 381st Bomb Group hold a close formation during an operation over Europe in 1943–44. (USAAF)

9. Learn to anticipate changes in position so that only slight control corrections are necessary. Large corrections and constant fighting of the controls quickly wear out even a strong pilot.
10. Keep the airplane properly trimmed to compensate for consumed fuel, crew movement, released bombs, etc. A poorly trimmed airplane is difficult to hold in position.
11. Do not use only the outboard engines to maintain position; use all 4 engines.
12. Always enter a formation from below, which is preferable, or from the same level, but never from above.

★★★

The B-25 Mitchell was a very different animal compared to a "heavy" like a B-24 or B-17. Unlike the heavy bombers, the twin-engine Mitchell was comparatively fast and agile, and was thus used in a wider spectrum of combat mission types, from conventional medium-altitude formation bombing through to low-level strafing and fragmentation bomb runs against enemy land positions, and from "skip-bombing" shipping to anti-submarine patrols. Although Mitchells did serve in the ETO, the defining theater for the B-25 was the Pacific Theater of Operations (PTO). As its variants progressed, the Mitchell came to be equipped with the most extraordinary armament: the B-25H carried 12–18 .50-cal (12.7mm) machine guns and a thumping 75mm T13E1 cannon, the latter mounted alongside four .50-cals in the nose, plus 3,000lb of bombs, another 2,000lb of ordnance (including torpedoes) on external hardpoints, and racks of eight 5in high-velocity aircraft rockets (HVAR). The following extract from the pilot training manual for the B-25 reminds us that bomber pilots and copilots in World War II performed many types of missions, each with its own inherent risks and demands on the skills of the flier.

From *Pilot Training Manual for the Mitchell Bomber B-25* (1945)

Some Typical Missions
FORMATION BOMBING

1. This is a day, 6-ship formation bombing mission. A Norden sight will be used in the lead ship on each element and D-8 sights will

be used in wing ships. Bombardiers in lead ships will sight for both range and deflection. Bombardiers in wing ships will drop bombs on lead ship.

2. Flight leader will take off at a predetermined time; other ships will take off at 30 second intervals and join formation.

3. After formation has been satisfactorily joined, one circle will be made of the field. During this circle, formation will climb at 170 mph.

4. Flight leader should have an approximate power setting of 32" MP at 2200 rpm. Climb will continue on course until an altitude of 10,000 feet is obtained. High blower will **not** be used and all ships will keep mixture controls in "FULL RICH" position.

5. Upon reaching the desired altitude, the leader will assume that antiaircraft fire has been encountered, and evasive action will be used.

6. Upon approaching the target, a gentle left turn, diving at 1000 feet per minute onto the target, will be executed. This final turn requires judgment and precision timing on the part of the lead ship. After diving to the correct bombing altitude (8000 feet), and onto the target, the lead ship should be in a position to 166 allow approximately a 20 second bomb run, straight and level. Immediately upon the closing of the bomb bay doors, the leader will again make a left turn, diving at 1000 feet per minute with a bank not to exceed 15 degrees. This dive will be held until 7000 feet altitude is reached. The following data should be strictly observed:

   A. The lead ship should climb at 170 MPH, with approximate power settings of 32" MP and 2200 RPM. The wing ships should use 2400 RPM.

   B. After altitude is reached, power settings of lead ship should not exceed 1900 RPM and 27" at any time. The wing ships should use at least 2000 RPM.

   C. Copilots must be sure that RPM is increased if the MP dictates it.

   D. The bombing run should be made at an indicated airspeed of 230 MPH, and upon leaving the target, should not exceed 250 MPH.

E. Wing ships will open bomb bay doors immediately upon seeing doors of lead ship open, and bombs will be dropped on the lead ship. **The Bombardier-Navigator must be quick in releasing bombs after he sees the first bomb leave the lead ship**.

F. Caution must be used by the lead ship at all times. Turns and maneuvers must be gone into gently and slowly.

G. After bombing is completed, flight will return to home base and break up into three-ship elements for landing.

GUNNERY MISSION

1. In this and all ensuing gunnery missions when both ground and water targets are used, extreme care must be exercised to see that the field of fire is clear of other planes.

Instructions for Firing
Ground Targets

A. Five rounds of 75MM ammunition from a range of 2000 yards, firing one round on each approach, plane to turn away from target immediately after firing while using additional evasive action.

B. Five rounds of 75MM ammunition from a range of 2000 yards, firing one round on each approach, using evasive action before and after reaching the 2000-yard point. Approach from 1000 yards and until passing over the target will be covered with short intermittent bursts of 50-Caliber fire.

Water Targets

A. Eleven rounds of 75MM ammunition from a range of 3000 yards, firing one round on each approach, plane to turn away from target immediately after firing while using additional evasive action.

2. The following course will be flown to and from Gunnery Range at a minimum altitude of 200 feet above the terrain. Flight will be made in 2- or 3-ship formations. Formation will go into column for gunnery.

B-25 After-action Report

The following Pacific Theater combat account came from Second Lieutenant Ivan Head. Titled "Tactical Study of Attack on Convoy Near Lae, New Guinea," it was dated March 10, 1943. In it he explains low-level "skip-bombing" tactics used by B-25s against Japanese shipping:

> Various types of approach were made by the B-25C-1s. Some letting down to about 500 to 200 feet and then lowering to masthead elevation about 4 to 600 yards from the target. Others made for water surface immediately and stayed at this elevation for the entire run on the target. Each aircraft began strafing the target from about 1000 yards and continued strafing until about 100 yards away. Emphasis should be placed on the fact that in every case the intensity of the fire from the enemy vessels was decreased when the B-25C-1s opened fire on them. The bombing run made by each aircraft was at an altitude of about 10 to 15 feet at an average speed of about 250 MPH. In most cases the bombs were toggled in rapid succession in order that one bomb would skip into the side of the vessel attacked and the other bomb would be placed on the deck. This method of releasing the bombs almost positively assures a hit. If the first bomb falls short of the target, the second bomb will skip into the side of the vessel and if the target is overshot slightly the first bomb will, in most cases, fall upon the deck of the vessel. In the attack on the morning of March 3, every aircraft that released its bombs scored a direct hit and in many cases two direct hits, on one bombing run. 37 bombs were dropped with 17 hits observed. 500 lb 5 sec. delay bombs were used.

[. . .]

CHEMICAL SPRAY MISSION

1. This is a chemical mission, using MR [Molasses residuum] and FS [Sulfur trioxide and chlorosulfuric acid].
2. The plane will be equipped for the mission with a bomb bay chemical spray tank containing MR and two chemical wing tanks—one on each wing—containing FS.
3. The MR target for the mission will be the X Target. The FS target will be the Z target.

4. The MR target is located approximately in the middle of the target area and is marked by **an orange cross in its center**.

5. Chemical tanks will be loaded into the plane. Plane will then be flown to the Z target, making an attack with FS, using one wing tank, from an altitude of 100 ft. normally, with the intention of covering the center of the target with a screen of smoke.

6. The plane will then fly to X target, making an attack with MR from an altitude of 150 ft. after inspecting the field to see that the target is in place.

7. The plane will then return to Z target and release the second smoke screen from the remaining FS wing tank.

8. All crew members will be equipped with gas masks while in the performance of this mission. Copilot will wear gas mask beginning 30 seconds before release of chemical until ship has been landed and brought to a stop.

9. This mission will not be flown when the wind velocity is greater than 20 mph.

10. Magnetic course to X target, 197 degrees; distance 50 miles.

11. Special attention should be given to direction of wind. Chemicals should be dropped from a flight path perpendicular to the wind.

12. Mission will be flown at 500 feet above terrain. Towns along route will be avoided.

13. The crew will be interrogated upon return to Home Base as to results of the mission.

DAY NAVIGATION, PHOTO-RECONNAISSANCE, AND INSTRUMENT LET-DOWN MISSION

1. This mission will consist of a controlled ground speed day navigation and photo-reconnaissance mission, at the end of which the pilot will orient himself by the X Radio Range and simulate a let-down to Home Base. If first attempt is unsuccessful, a second orientation and let-down will be accomplished.

2. **Conduct of Mission:**
   A. This mission will be briefed by the Squadron S-2. All crew members will take careful notes as directed by S-2, and will be interrogated upon return as to observation. Oblique and

pinpoint photographs will be taken. Target maps are available for the localities directed below and photographs will be taken of each given target.

3. **Specific Duties of Crew Members:**
   A. Pilot-will aid and direct crew in obtaining observations; give careful attention to best photographic procedures;

Armorers load up belts of .50-caliber ammunition for a Browning M2A1 machine gun in the nose of a North American B-25 Mitchell at Hawkins Field on Betio Island, Tarawa, in 1943. (USGOV-PD)

direct photographs be taken as briefed; and communicate on interphone at all times.

B. Copilot—will take notes on installation noted by himself and pilot and accomplish all normal copilot duties.

C. Navigator-Bombardier

(1) Will navigate by DR Navigation on a V-P chart except within 10 minutes of target area where pinpoint pilotage will be used on a sectional chart.

(2) Act as observer and perform duties as briefed by S-2.

(3) Maintain and submit navigation log, weather observations, and other data to Squadron Navigation Officer.

D. Radio Operator—will transmit position reports submitted by Bombardier-Navigator, and practice tracking from all gun positions.

E. Engineer-Gunner—will perform all normal duties and also act as observer.

F. Armorer-Gunner—will preflight and install photo equipment; take photos as directed by pilot; make observations of ground activity; and man battle station at all times, taking careful observations and reporting to the pilot all aircraft and ground installations sighted.

★★★

Of all the heavy bombers in the USAAF, it was the B-17 Flying Fortress that generally had the most appeal to those aspiring to become bomber pilots. Indeed, the B-24 Liberator—the nearest competitor to the B-17—was sometimes disparagingly referred to as "the crate the B-17 came in." Closer and fuller comparison between the B-17 and B-24 demolishes many of the myths. The B-24 was just as powerful as the B-17 (indeed it was faster), had a heavier bombload, was equally rugged, and had greater operational versatility. In reality, the only area in which the B-24 fell short was that it attracted less media coverage than the B-17. Nevertheless, the B-17 Flying Fortress was indeed an astonishing weapon of war: a 10-man aircraft that (in its B-17G variant) could haul 4,500lb (2,000 kg) of bombs to a long-range target (its bombload could be nearly doubled for a short-range target) while protecting itself with a total of 13 turret-mounted or flexible .50-cal M2 Browning machine guns. The following text from a B-17 pilot training manual provides some technical insights into what the B-17 was like to fly. Much of B-17: Pilot Training Manual for the Flying Fortress is extremely technical, reminding us that the USAAF pilots and copilots were of necessity individuals of advanced intelligence.

From *B-17: Pilot Training Manual for the Flying Fortress* (1944)

FLIGHT CHARACTERISTICS

The B-17F possesses many outstanding flight characteristics, chief among which are: (1) directional stability; (2) strong aileron effect in turns; (3) ability to go around without change in elevator trim; (4) exceptionally satisfactory stalling characteristics; and (5) extremely effective elevator control in takeoff and landing.

Trim Tabs

The airplane will go around without changes in elevator trim tab settings. However, trim must be changed with adjustment of cowl flaps and power settings, for these reasons:

1. Increased power on the inboard engines causes the airplane to become slightly tail-heavy. (Power change on the outboard engines has no appreciable effect on trim.)
2. Closing the cowl flaps on the inboard engines also causes tail-heaviness. (The effect of cowl flaps on the outboards is negligible.)

With the airplane properly trimmed for a power-off, flaps-down landing, you can take off and go around again by applying power and putting the flap switch "UP" with no change in trim. The flaps will retract at a satisfactorily slow rate.

Turns

Because of the inherent directional stability of the B-17, dropping one wing will produce a noticeable turning effect. Very little rudder and aileron will enable you to roll in and out of turns easily. Carefully avoid uncoordinated use of aileron.

In shallow turns the load factors are negligible. But in steeper turns proportionately more back pressure is required, thereby increasing the load factor.

In banks from 10° to 70° the load factor increases from 1.5 to 3.0. Obviously, steep turns of a heavily loaded airplane may place sufficient stress on the wings to cause structural failure.

If the airplane tends to slip out of turns, recover smoothly without attempting to hold bank. Decrease the bank. Use proper coordination of rudder and aileron.

Rough Air Operation

In rough air, use both rudder and ailerons without worrying about excessive loads. Both aileron and rudder forces vary with changes in airspeed in such manner that it is almost impossible to damage the system without deliberately trying to do so. Necessary control pressures are small enough, and the responses large enough, to maintain ample control of the airplane.

However, in the case of the elevators, exercise great care, both in rough air and in recovery from dives, to assure smooth operation. In thunderstorms, squalls, and in or near turbulent cumulus clouds, it is possible to develop excessive load factors by means of the elevators unless they are used properly. This does not mean that there is any greater tendency to exceed allowable load factors in the B-17 than in other heavy bombardment or transport airplanes. It means that **the larger the airplane, the greater the time and distance required to complete any maneuver**. In operation, you must allow more distance and time in proportion to the size of the airplane.

Generally, in rough air, hold constant airspeed by means of the elevator, but do it smoothly. Remember that recovery to the desired airspeed may take time.

Avoid hurried recovery from dives, climbs or changes in airspeed. Never dive the airplane through a cloud layer or through rough air at maximum diving speed. Don't attempt high-speed flight in rough air.

Stalls

The stall characteristics of the B-17 are highly satisfactory. The tendency to roll—commonly caused by lack of symmetry in the stalling of either wing—is minimized by the large vertical tail. Under all conditions a stall warning at several mph above stalling speed is indicated by buffeting of the elevators.

If airspeed is reduced rapidly near the stall, the speed at which the stall will occur will be lower than when the stall is approached gradually. The stall will also be more violent because the wing's angle of attack will be considerably above the stalling attitude.

The stalling speed of the B-17F, like that of any other airplane, depends upon: (a) the gross weight, (b) the load factor (number of Gs), (c) the wing flap setting, (d) the power, (e) de-icer operation and ice formation.

The effect of gross weight upon stalling speed is obvious: the heavier the load, the higher the stalling speed.

The effect of the load factor is simply to increase the effective gross weight in proportion to the load factor.

The greater the flap angle the lower the stalling speed. The greater the power, the lower the stalling speed. Full flaps reduce the stalling speed about 15 mph for gross weights of 40,000 to 45,000 lb., and a load factor of 1.0; but full military power for the same loading conditions may reduce the stalling speed another 15 mph.

Any yawing, accidental or otherwise, will increase the stalling speed and any tendency to roll at the stall. This is obvious, since the normal procedure in deliberately making a spin is to yaw the airplane as it stalls. For example, if the left wing drops at the stall and you apply right aileron to raise the left wing, the ailerons will have a tendency to overbalance and reverse effectiveness, because of the drag induced by the aileron. The result will be increased dropping of the left wing. The aileron procedure in recovering from a stall, therefore, is to **hold ailerons neutral and refrain from their use until coming out of the dive in the final phase of recovery**.

Stall Recovery

For the B-17F the procedure for recovering from a stall is normal.

1. Regain airspeed for normal flight by smooth operation of the elevators. This may require a dive up to 30°.
2. While regaining airspeed, use rudder to maintain laterally level flight. After airspeed is regained, use ailerons also for lateral control but not until airspeed is regained.

The important thing is to **recover from the dive smoothly**. Penalty for failure to make a smooth recovery may be a secondary stall or structural damage to the airplane, both because of excessive load factors. Rough or abrupt use of elevators to regain normal flying 90 speed may cause the dive to become excessively steep.

The additional airspeed necessary to regain normal flight need not be more than 20 mph.

This means that excessive diving to regain airspeed is absolutely unnecessary.

Remember these additional facts about stalls:

1. Stalls with wheels down will increase the stalling speed about 5 mph.
2. Stalls with wheels and flaps down will decrease the stalling speed about 10 mph.
3. Stalls with de-icer boots operating will increase the stalling speed 10–15 mph. In recovering from stalls with de-icer boots operating, regain slightly more than the usual 20 mph needed for recovery. Such stalls are apt to be more abrupt, with a greater tendency to roll.

Spins

Accidental spinning of the B-17 is extremely unlikely. The directional stability and damping are great, and it is probable that even a deliberate spin would be difficult. However, remember that the airplane was not designed for spinning, and deliberate spins are forbidden.

Dives

The maximum permissible diving speed in the B-17F (flaps and wheels up) with modified elevators is 270 mph IAS; without elevator modifications, the maximum diving speed is 220 mph.

The structural factors limiting the diving speed of the B-17F are the engine ring cowl strength, the wing leading-edge de-icer boot strength, the cockpit windshield and canopy strength, and the critical flutter speed. The engine ring cowl has been designed to withstand 420 mph. The windshield and cockpit canopy have ample margin at 305 mph. The wing leading-edge de-icer boots begin to raise slightly from the wing at 305 mph, and any additional speed would be likely to lift the upper part of the boot above the wing surface, possibly causing structural failure. The mass balance of the control surface is so essentially complete both statically and dynamically that, basically, the critical flutter speed depends entirely on the wing-bending torsion critical speed, which is approximately 375 mph.

Therefore, it is obvious that simply diving the airplane (with modified elevators) to 270 mph involves no danger whatsoever. The only danger that must be considered is in recovery. Recovery must be smooth and gradual. Normally, a load factor of 2 will not be exceeded.

At the gross weight of 50,000 lb., the initial yield point factor is slightly less than 3, making the ultimate load factor slightly over 4. Obviously, at that gross weight the load factor 3 should never be reached; the load factor 2 normally will not be exceeded.

Heavy Loads

The B-17 is stable longitudinally with heavy loads as long as the center of gravity is forward of 32% of the Mean Aerodynamic Chord (87 inches aft of the leading edge of the center section).

For all normal loading the CG [center of gravity] must be kept forward of 32% of the MAC [mean aerodynamic chord]. If an excessive load is placed in the rear, the airplane will have neutral or negative stability. It is possible to trim the airplane with an unstable load, but it will be difficult to fly, especially on instruments. It is also much easier to stall inadvertently when flying an unstable airplane on instruments.

Loading for the forward CG positions is preferred because, in addition to being easier to fly, it gives a smooth increase in elevator forces required to pull out of dives and eliminates the necessity of using excessive elevator trim to hold the tail up.

Straggler after Kassel Raid

The following first-hand account was published in November 1943 in Air Force. *It is a report written by First Lieutenant James J. Maginnis, the pilot of B-17* Positionality, *who unemotionally explains the formidable persistence of his crew during a raid over Kassel and the intensifying challenges of reaching home:*

We took off on a flight to Germany, flying in the second element of the high squadron of the high group in a three group combat wing. We formed and ascended without trouble and saw a few fighters and a little flak as we crossed the coast going in.

Things went well until forty minutes from the target when the manifold pressure on No. 4 engine suddenly dropped to twelve and stayed there. We manipulated turbo control, throttle, mixture, rpm and cowl flaps, but could get no rise from the turbo. It was quite evident that either the turbo regulator or the turbo itself was gone. The engine was left running since it wasn't holding us back too much, and a feathered engine is always an invitation to enemy fighters. We determined to reach the target so long as they didn't cause us to lose the formation.

At this time Sergeant McCurdy, the left waist gunner, reported that the flaps had crept down four to five inches. This was indicated in the cockpit but the flaps would not retract electrically. The waist gunner was ordered to crank them up and bind the handle in place. This was done, though the flaps remained slightly down.

We stayed with the formation on three engines until about ten minutes before the target when No. 4 engine began to throw oil and smoke very badly. At this point, we feathered it.

The target was reached OK and our bombs were dropped from close formation. With the help of Second Lieut. William J. Holloway, the navigator, the turns from the target and rally point were anticipated and utilized to keep us in close to the formation.

Right after the target we began totalling the gas and found the greatest amount was 95 gallons in No. 1 tank. It was evident we would have entirely too little gas to complete the mission as scheduled. Tech. Sgt. William A. Glenn, the top turret gunner, was ordered to transfer fuel from No. 4 to No. 1 tank since No. 1 was the lowest. He set the fuel transfer valves and pump but after fifteen minutes it was evident that no gas was leaving No. 4 tank. The pump fuse was checked and found OK. No hand transfer pump was installed.

It was necessary to use full power all the way out to stay with the formation in its evasive action against flak. When possible we climbed up into the high squadron on the inside of turns, and when necessary we dropped down into the lead or low squadron on the outside of turns.

Then as we approached the coast, No. 1 began cutting out for lack of gas causing us to drop behind the formation. We dove to try and catch the low squadron, and at this time I first heard the plane being peppered with bullets and shells. We could not catch the low squadron so I dove for the group below us.

An explosive shell hit the oxygen, throwing splinters into pilot and copilot, filling the cockpit with smoke and dust a starting a fire. Although not wounded, Lieutenant Holloway and Second Lieut. Edward C. Piech, the bombardier, were knocked down and stunned. The co-pilot put the fire out with a fire extinguisher. Simultaneously, the bomb bay doors swung open, the flaps went down one-third, and No. 1 engine stopped putting out and was feathered.

I started diving at 250–300 mph and over 6,000 feet per minute, taking evasive action, while heading for a layer of strata cumulus clouds at 5,000. Near the cloud layer, with No. 1 and No. 4 engines feathered, orders were given to prepare for ditching. In the cloud layer a course of 275 degrees was taken and soon No. 3 engine ran out of gas and was feathered. Altitude was lost to 3,000 feet, where we broke out below the cloud. The fighters had left us.

No. 4 engine was unfeathered and was found to put out full power but no turbo boost. Airspeed was kept at 110–120 to maintain 3,000 feet altitude. All preparations had been made for ditching. SOSs and QDMs were going out OK. Sergeant McCurdy, badly wounded, was in the radio room being treated.

We sighted the English coast about ten miles ahead. As we crossed the coast at 3,000 feet, No. 2 engine began to falter, and soon thereafter was feathered. That left No. 4 doing all the work.

A few miles inland we spotted an airport under construction. We examined the control cables and surfaces and found them satisfactory for any landing. The wheels were put down, and we stayed between the coast and airport so a ditching or beach landing could be made if wheels fully or partially failed to extend.

Two of the three runways hid large obstructions on them but the third had only minor obstructions such as barrels and bales of wire. The wheels and tires were down and checked, so an approach was made with the crew in position for crash landing. The landing was made and immediately the right tire began to get flat. The ship was kept on the runway with left brake and No. 1 engine, the only unfeathered engine. About thirty gallons of gas were left in No. 4.

Perfect cooperation was achieved by the whole crew. Every man did his assigned job throughout and all obeyed orders quickly and accurately.

In the few minutes of running fight Sergeant Reeder, the tail gunner, shot down two enemy fighters: Sergeant Long, the ball turret gunner, shot down another, and Sergeant McCurdy a fourth after he had received his mortal wound.

CHAPTER 3

Bombardier

The bombardier's responsibilities were absolutely central to the entire purpose of a bomber aircraft—it was his job to put ordnance on target. To the uninitiated, this might suggest little more than laying some crosshairs on the intended target and flicking the bomb-release switch, but in reality, the bombardier performed a job with exceptional intellectual and mental demands, reflected in the fact that bombardier school lasted a full 20 weeks. The bombardier had to use technology, mathematics, physics, and judgement to solve the "bombing problem"—how to put an inert piece of ordnance onto a small target from altitudes of 15,000–25,000ft, allowing for factors such as gravity, airspeed, air resistance, wind, altitude, angle of approach, the weather, and multiple other influences. Although there were popular claims that bombers could drop bombs into a "pickle barrel," these claims were usually made by bombsight manufacturers. In reality, World War II bombing was generally grossly inaccurate. A study of USAAF bombing accuracy in 1943 found that even in good weather conditions, only 13 percent of bombs actually fell within 1,000ft of the assigned Mean Point of Impact (MPI). This being said, using precision bombsights such as the Norden "S" and the Sperry "S" series, bombardiers were still able to get bombs close to or on their targets, the spread of bombs falling from the wider formation compensating to some degree for individual inaccuracies.

The following passage, from Pilot Training Manual for the B-24 Liberator, *usefully explains to bomber pilots what it is that the bombardier does. Buried in the list is the fact that the bombardier was also a gunner, operating firepower at the front of the aircraft. But once the bomber reached its "Initial Point" (IP)—the beginning of the bomb run—it would be the bombardier in charge, staring at the world below through a bombsight while calmly but quickly making the calculations for the perfect moment of bomb release.*

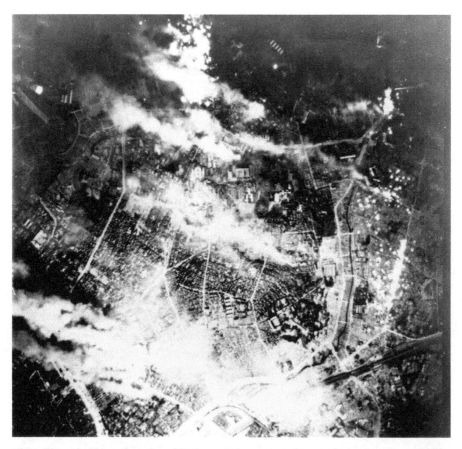

Tokyo burns under a devastating U.S. incendiary bombing attack on May 26, 1945. By the end of the air campaign against Tokyo in August 1945, an estimated 80,000–130,000 of the city's civilian population had been killed. (LOC)

From *Pilot Training Manual for the B-24 Liberator* (1945)

THE BOMBARDIER

Accurate and effective bombing is the ultimate purpose of your entire airplane and crew. Every other function is preparatory to hitting and destroying the target.

That's your bombardier's job. The success or failure of the mission depends upon what he accomplishes in the short interval of the bombing run.

When the bombardier takes over the airplane for the run on the target, he is in command. He will tell you what he wants done, and until he gives you the word "Bombs away," his word is virtually law.

A great deal, therefore depends on the understanding between bombardier and pilot. You expect your bombardier to know his job when he takes over. He expects you to understand the problems involved in his job, and to give him full cooperation. Teamwork between pilot and bombardier is essential.

Under any given set of conditions, ground speed, altitude, direction, etc., there is only one point in space where a bomb may be released from the airplane to hit a predetermined object on the ground.

There are many things with which a bombardier must be thoroughly familiar in order to release his bombs at the right point to hit this predetermined target.

He must know and understand his bombsight, what it does, and how it does it.

He must thoroughly understand the operation and upkeep of his bombing instruments and equipment.

He must know that his racks, switches, controls, releases, doors, linkage, etc., are in first-class operating condition.

He must understand the automatic pilot as it pertains to bombing.

He must know how to set it up, make air adjustments and minor repairs while in flight.

He must know how to operate all gun positions in the airplane.

He must know how to load and how to clear simple stoppages and jams of guns in flight.

He must be able to load and fuse his own bombs.

He must understand the destruction power of bombs and must know the vulnerable spots on various types of targets.

He must understand the bombing problem, bombing probabilities, bombing errors, etc.

He must be thoroughly versed in target identification and in aircraft identification.

The bombardier should be familiar with the duties of all members of the crew and should be able to assist the navigator in case the navigator becomes incapacitated.

For the bombardier to be able to do his job, the pilot of the aircraft must place the aircraft in the proper position to arrive at a point on a circle about the target from which the bombs can be released to hit the target.

Unless the pilot performs his part of the bombing run correctly, even the best bombardier in the world will be unable to bomb accurately. The pilot's failure to hold airspeed and altitude will cause the following bombing errors:

The bombardier of a B-17 Flying Fortress mans a flexible MG armament. The pulley system attached to the heavy Browning machine guns made them easier to move and aim accurately, especially at altitude when muscular strength was reduced. (USAF)

1. Flying too high: bomb will hit over.
2. Flying too low: bomb will fall short.
3. Flying too fast: bomb will fall short.
4. Flying too slow: bomb will hit over.

★★★

The bomb run was a tense and perilous time in a combat mission. It required that the bomber fly a predictable, straight line from the IP to the bomb release point, sometimes for up to 30 minutes or more. Predictability was, of course, a gift to enemy fighter aircraft and antiaircraft gunners, as it enabled them to make more accurate attacks, fine-tuning their fire until they brought it onto target. Furthermore, the bomb run required that the bomb doors of the aircraft be opened; during the USAAF daylight bombing raids, these open doors could be seen from the ground through powerful optics, thus the antiaircraft fire would intensify horrifically in the attempt to disrupt the bombing accuracy. The bombardier would, depending on the aircraft, often take over control of the bomb run flight path through the Automatic Flight Control Equipment (AFCE), which slaved lateral movement of the aircraft to the bombardier's bombsight controls (the pilot still had control of airspeed and altitude). It would require exceptional concentration for the bombardier to fine-tune the approach to target, his eye glued to the bombsight optic, while enemy fighters and antiaircraft fire did everything they could to destroy the aircraft he rode in.

From *Bombardier's Information File* (1944)

CREW COORDINATION
BOMBARDIER TO CREW

Cooperate with pilot: Explain to him the principles of the bombing problem. Emphasize importance of not changing altitude or airspeed radically during bombing run and of informing you before reaching bomb release point if altitude or airspeed is off. Tactfully assist him in preflight and adjustment of autopilot. Give him information on other aircraft ahead and below; talk him into formation. Report flak bursts and frontal fighter attacks.

Cooperate with navigator: Explain bombardiering to him so that he can assume role of bombardier in an emergency. Help in DR [dead reckoning] and pilotage navigation. Obtain drift and groundspeed from bombsight. Warn of approach of bad weather.

Cooperate with armament crew: Report accurately and promptly any malfunction of bombsight or other bombing equipment. Assist them in preflight of bomb racks and controls, and in loading and fusing bombs. Assist in flight checking autopilot.

Cooperate with gunners: Assist in loading ammunition, and in preflight of guns and ammunition. Inform them of frontal fighter attacks at which they best can fire. When using remote control turrets, maintain closest coordination in transferring control.

Cooperate with radar operator: Explain the bombing problem to him; stress importance of supplying accurate data for bombing run. When visibility permits, give him check points and keep him informed of his accuracy. Work in closest coordination when bombing through overcast; notify him if visibility allows you to take over bombing run.

CREW TO BOMBARDIER

Pilot and copilot cooperate with you: They must coordinate closely in obtaining pre-set data, in making turn over IP [initial point], and in taking evasive action. They must adjust autopilot to obtain maximum performance for bombing. Pilot should not jockey airspeed or change altitude radically during bombing run. Before reaching bomb release point, they should notify you if altitude or airspeed is off. Pilot must make prompt but smooth, coordinated turns in following PDI [pilot direction indicator].

Navigator cooperates with you: He should explain navigation to you, so that you can assume role of navigator in an emergency. He should check your computations of true airspeed, bombing altitude, wind, groundspeed, and drift. Navigator should check trail and disc speed found from bombing tables and set into bombsight. He helps to identify IP and target. On the bombing run navigator gives you the variations of airspeed and altitude and assists in making computations for offset bombing.

Armament crew cooperates with you: They assist in preflight of bomb racks and controls. They must load and fuse bombs carefully and accurately. Armament crew ground checks autopilot. They must maintain bombsight, bomb racks and controls, auto-pilot, guns and turrets with care and thoroughness and keep them in best possible condition.

Gunners cooperate with you: They assist in loading ammunition and in preflight of guns and ammunition. They report frontal attacks at which you best can fire. Gunners should report bomb rack malfunctions and bomb hit data.

Radar operator cooperates with you: He must work in close coordination with you on bombing run, especially when bombing through overcast. He should give you accurate information on check points, drift, bombing altitude, groundspeed, dropping angle.

[. . .]

BOMBING PROBLEM

The moment a bomb is released from an airplane it encounters several forces. These forces are: gravity, true airspeed, air resistance, and wind. The combined effect of these forces determines the path (trajectory) that the bomb follows and where it hits. Gravity pulls the bomb toward the earth at a continually increasing speed. It exerts the same force on all bombs, whatever their size, shape, or weight. Since the bomb is part of the airplane up to the instant of release, it leaves it with the forward speed of the airplane. This forward speed of airplane and bomb relative to air is **true airspeed (TAS)**.

Trail

Air resists the bomb in its flight and acts against the forces of gravity and TAS. This resistance keeps the bomb in flight longer and decreases its forward speed through the air. Thus, it lags behind the airplane. The horizontal distance that it lags is its **trail**. Trail, consequently, is the horizontal distance measured on the ground from the point of impact to a point directly beneath the airplane at the instant of impact.

Remember that trail is the result of several forces acting upon the bomb. While TAS drives the bomb forward, air resistance tends to hold it back. While gravity pulls it down, air resistance tends to hold it up. When TAS increases, the horizontal resistance of the air increases; thus, trail is greater. Similarly, when the downward speed of the bomb increases, the vertical resistance of the air increases and trail is greater. The downward speed of the bomb depends on the height of the airplane above the target, that is, the **bombing altitude (BA)** from which the bomb is dropped.

The amount of resistance which the air offers to the bomb also depends on its size, shape, and weight. Ordnance engineers classify a bomb according to its ballistic coefficient (Ball. Coeff.), the relative amount of resistance the air offers to it. A bomb with a high ballistic coefficient falls faster and with less trail than a bomb with a low ballistic coefficient. The amount of trail for each bomb at practical BA and TAS ranges has been determined by tests and is given in your bombing tables.

Trail increases as $\begin{cases} \text{BA increases} \\ \text{TAS increases} \\ \text{Ball. Coeff. decreases} \end{cases}$

Wind

In addition to the forces of gravity, TAS, and air resistance, **wind** acts upon the bomb during its flight and affects the trajectory. Think of wind as the movement of the mass of air in which the airplane is flying. Wind does not affect the TAS of the airplane. Therefore, it has no effect on trail, since trail depends only on TAS, BA, and type of bomb.

Headwinds or tailwinds do affect the **groundspeed (GS)** of the airplane. When there is a tailwind, it increases GS. Therefore, you must release the bomb at a greater distance from the target in order to hit it. Conversely, when there is a headwind, you must release the bomb closer to the target.

When there is a crosswind, **drift** enters the bombing problem. To compensate for drift, you bead the airplane into the wind sufficiently to

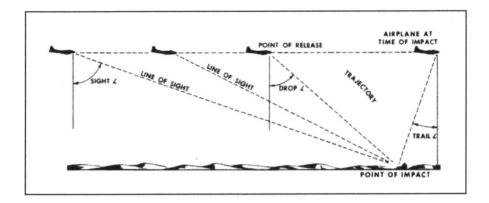

make good a course the proper distance upwind of the target. This distance that the airplane must fly upwind of the target is **crosstrail (CT)**. In other words, CT is the distance that the bomb is carried downwind while it is falling.

Actual Time of Fall

The time factor you must know to solve the range problem is the **actual time of fall (ATF)** of the bomb. It is the time that elapses between the release and impact of the ATF.

ATF depends primarily on BA but it is affected also by TAS and bomb ballistics. If air resistance did not affect the fall of the bomb you could find the approximate ATF by the equation, Time = ¼ $\sqrt{BA}$. Since air does retard the fall of the bomb, ATF for each type of bomb at practical BA and TAS ranges had to be found by actual tests and is given in your bombing tables.

You set ATF into the M-series bombsight as a **disc speed (DS)**. You can find DS by dividing ATF into **5300**, the **bombsight constant**. Thus DS = 5300/ATF. DS for each type of bomb through practical BA and TAS ranges also is given in your bombing tables.

DS decreases as $\left\{ \begin{array}{l} \text{BA increases} \\ \text{TAS increases} \\ \text{Ball. Coeff. decreases} \end{array} \right.$

Ranges

Groundspeed is the **rate** factor you must know to solve the range problem. When you synchronize, your bombsight solves for GS and combines it with ATF to find the distance, **whole range (WR)**. WR is the horizontal distance the airplane travels during ATF. You can find it by the equation,

WR (ft) = ATF (sec) × GS (ft/sec)

Since the bomb lags trail distance behind the airplane, you subtract trail from WR to find **actual range (A)**. Thus AR = WR − Trail. AR is the horizontal distance the bomb travels during ATF.

Angles

When you look at the target through the bombsight optics, you look along an imaginary line from the bombsight to the target. **This is the line of sight**.

The axis of the vertical gyro is the vertical line of reference the bombsight uses in solving the bombing problem. This reference may or may not be in the **true vertical**, perpendicular to the earth. Only if you level the bubbles perfectly do you establish the gyro axis in the true vertical.

The angle between the bombsight vertical reference and the line of sight at any instant is the **sighting angle (Sight ∠)**. As the airplane approaches the target, the line of sight sweeps toward the vertical and the Sight L decreases toward 0°.

The particular Sight ∠ set up by the bombsight at the instant of bomb release is the **dropping angle (Drop ∠)**. The Drop ∠ is the angle between line of sight and bombsight vertical reference at the instant of bomb release. The Sight ∠ and the Drop ∠ are measured from the bombsight vertical reference you set up, whether it is the true vertical or not.

The angle between the line of sight and the true vertical at any instant is the **range angle (Range ∠)**. It differs from the Sight ∠ by the amount the bombsight vertical reference is out of true vertical. The angle that subtends the AR of the bomb is the **actual range angle (AR ∠)**. If the bombing problem has been solved properly and the vertical reference set up is in the true vertical, the Drop ∠ is the same as the AR ∠ and subtends the AR of the bomb. The angle that subtends the WR is the **whole range angle (WR ∠)**. The angle that subtends trail is the **trail angle (Trail ∠)**. Trail is given and used in terms of mils.

[. . .]

"Air Discipline"

The article "Air Discipline" was written by Brigadier General Frank A. Armstrong, Jr., who held numerous commands within USAAF bomber forces during World War II. In this extract, we sense the grit behind his belief in the authority of the bombardier during the run to target:

We fly a fairly tight formation, but each bomber is assigned a block of air within which he may maneuver and alter his speed and altitude depending on the situation and the type of attack It is vital that each pilot understand how much freedom he is allowed and how far he can go without stepping out of formation.

When a plane drops out, it not only jeopardizes its own position but takes twelve guns away from the formation. And when a plane is shot up and starts falling behind we have to let it go. We can't send more planes to stick with it. That would weaken our main effort. It's not easy to continue on your way when you see a ship drop out and know that enemy fighters swarm over a straggler like ants on a fallen sparrow. We do everything we possibly can to save every ship and bring them all back, but air discipline demands that we protect the group.

Knowing that we bomb as a group, the enemy tries to knock down the lead plane. He thinks that is his best bet. But to date the Hun has never turned back a formation. We don't turn back! And we don't jettison bombs—no matter what happens.

The lead bombardier sights for range and deflection and the other planes follow his run. But every bombardier in the formation sets the data in his bombsight. He must be ready to take over in the event something goes wrong with the lead plane or his own ship is knocked out of formation.

During a bombing run, when the success of the whole mission depends on what is accomplished in a two- or three-minute interval, there is no time for formality or for recognition of rank. When the bombardier takes over the ship for the run on the target he is in command. I don't care what the relative rank between pilot and bombardier, the bombardier tells the pilot what he wants done. And he doesn't stand on any of the niceties of military etiquette. The bombardier *tells* him.

BOMB RACKS AND CONTROLS

The B-17 is widely used on bombing missions in all combat theaters. Typical of all bombers, it has been selected for the following explanation of how bomb racks and their controls operate. B-17 bomb racks and controls are not exactly like those of all other bombers but when you know how they operate you should understand the general operation of others.

The B-17 has both internal and external bomb racks. The internal racks have 42 stations and carry bombs ranging in weight from 100 lbs. to 2000 lbs. Each of the 42 stations is marked to show what weight bombs it can carry. There are 2 external bomb racks, one under each wing. Each can carry one bomb weighing from 1000 to 4000 lbs.

There are 2 kinds of bomb rack control systems, mechanical-electrical and all-electrical. In bombers which have the mechanical-electrical system you lock the racks, set up the A-2 release mechanisms for normal release, and salvo the bombs manually by means of control handles.

The all-electrical system is the newest type. When you are using it, you do not operate the A-4 release mechanisms manually. You make an emergency release (salvo) electrically. All manual controls have been eliminated.

Bombardier's Control Panel

The control panel in the bombardier's compartment contains the necessary switches for bomb release control, the bomb indicator lights, and the intervalometer. This panel is the electrical control center for releasing bombs. You must know every switch and how and when to use it.

The indicator light panel contains one light for each station on the bomb racks. To find out whether all indicator lights are operating, momentarily place the lamp test switch at MOM. All indicator lights should flash on. You can tell at a glance what stations in the bomb bay are loaded by turning the bomb indicator light switch ON for an instant. An indicator light shows for each A-4 bomb release mechanism that is cocked.

Normal Bomb Release (Train)

In train bombing, when you are using the all-electrical control system, make these necessary switch settings:

Master switch ON.

Bomb bay doors OPEN.

Desired rack selector switches ON. When bombs are released, they then drop in proper sequence. Bomb indicator light switch OFF and lamp test switch ON.

Arming switch ARMED, if you wish to drop bomb from external racks with an armed nose fuse.

Intervalometer train-select switch at TRAIN.

When the bombsight automatic release mechanism or bomb release switch completes the electrical circuit, an impulse is sent to the intervalometer. The intervalometer in turn sends out one impulse for each bomb to be released. As each release mechanism receives an impulse it operates the bomb shackle. The bomb is released armed.

To release bombs select, you must place the intervalometer train-select switch at SELECT. Set all other switches as you would for train bombing.

Emergency Release (Salvo)

You can release all internal and external bombs safe by placing any one of the 3 salvo switches at SALVO. The light beside each switch indicates that one or more of the salvo switches are closed. The closing of any one switch opens the bomb bay doors electrically in about 12 seconds. When the doors are completely open, an electrical impulse goes to the A-4 release mechanisms on the bomb racks. They operate the bomb shackles which salvo the bombs. The entire operation takes about 15 seconds. In the event of an electrical failure, you must open the bomb bay doors by means of a hand crank and release each bomb manually and individually.

The two external bombs are salvoed the instant the salvo switch closes. It is obvious that these racks are not dependent upon the bomb bay door being open. To salvo external bombs safe, place arming switch at SAFE. To salvo them armed, place arming switch at ARMED.

BOMB RELEASE MECHANISMS

The bomb release mechanism is an electrically operated mechanical device designed to cause the bomb shackle to release and arm a bomb.

A-4 Bomb Release

In order to release bombs, select or in train the bombardier's master switch must be ON, bomb bay doors OPEN, and the rack selection made. The electrical impulse from the bomb release switch or the bombsight automatic release mechanism energizes the rotary solenoid inside the A-4. The solenoid rotates to the select position, this trips the release lever and the arming lever.

Bombs are salvoed electrically, not manually. To salvo bombs place the salvo switch at SALVO. The solenoid rotates to the salvo position and only the release lever is tripped. To operate the A-4 manually, turn the trip screw (marked TRIP) on the front of the A-4 in the direction indicated. This affects the rotary solenoid like an electrical impulse, tripping both release lever and arming lever. When an A-4 has been cocked by mistake the trip screw permits tripping.

The fork of the release lever has one hinged ear. You can release bombs by prying the bomb shackle release lever over the hinged ear. This method of releasing a bomb safe is used when the A-4 is jammed, preventing normal operation.

Caution

The indicator light switch must be OFF while bombs are being released. If it is ON, a partial salvo results.

When release is tripped manually, trip screw should always be returned to vertical position or it will be impossible to cock release.

Do not apply current to solenoid continuously for more than 30 seconds.

A-2 Bomb Release

This bomb release has the same purpose as the A-4. In order to release bombs, the bombardier's master switch must be ON, bomb bay doors open, rack selection made, and release handle placed at SELECT. The electrical impulse operates the solenoid which first causes the arming lever and then the release lever to be tripped.

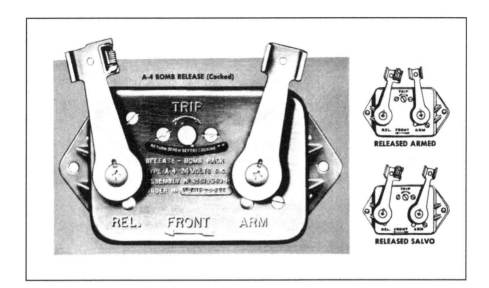

When using the A-2, you salvo the bombs manually. Place the release handle in your compartment at SALVO. This mechanically operates the release. The A-2, like the A-4, has a trip screw on the front and a hinged ear on the release lever.

[. . .]

SECTION 8   COMBAT BOMBING . . .

Bombardier's Checklist

The most carefully planned bombing mission can be ruined if the bombardier forgets an essential item of equipment or a vital step of procedure. A thorough check of equipment and steps is his only guarantee that he won't forget. This checklist is a valuable safeguard for his memory. It is not a guide to procedures.

BEFORE LOADING BOMBS

1. BOMB RACKS .... PREFLIGHTED
2. BOMBING INVERVALOMETER .... PREFLIGHTED
3. SWITCHES IN BOMBARDIER
   COMPARTMENT .... CHECKED

4. SWITCHES IN PILOT
    COMPARTMENT .... CHECKED
5. EMERGENCY RELEASE SYSTEM .... CHECKED
6. BOMB BAY SWITCHES .... OFF
7. NOSE COMPARTMENT .... CLEAR
8. WINDOWS .... CLEAN

BEFORE TAKEOFF

1. PERSONAL EQUIPMENT .... COMPLETE
2. BOMBARDIER'S KIT .... COMPLETE
3. TARGET FOLDER AND WEATHER
    DATA .... COMPLETE
4. OXYGEN AND MASK .... CHECKED
5. PARACHUTE AND LIFE VEST .... CHECKED
6. SPARE ELECTRICAL FUZES .... COMPLETE
7. BOMBS AND FUZES .... CHECKED
8. PINS (IF INACCESSIBLE IN FLIGHT) ...... PULLED
9. BOMB BAY TANK SAFETY
    SWITCHES .... OFF
10. INTERPHONE SYSTEM .... CHECKED
11. BOMBSIGHT .... PREFLIGHTED
12. AUTOPILOT .... PREFLIGHTED
13. GUNS, TURRETS, AND GUNSIGHTS .... PREFLIGHTED
14. CAMERA AND CAMERA
    INTERVALOMETER .... PREFLIGHTED
15. ALTIMETER PRESSURE SCALE
    AT 29.92 .... SET
16. CLOCK .... SYNCHRONIZED
17. SWITCHES IN BOMBARDIER
    COMPARTMENT .... OFF

BEFORE IP

1. SWITCHES IN PILOT
    COMPARTMENT .... CHECKED
2. SWITCHES IN BOMBARDIER
    COMPARTMENT .... CHECKED

3. All BOMBSIGHT SWITCHES .... ON
4. BOMB BAY SWITCHES .... CHECKED
5. PINS... PULLED
6. AUTOPILOT .... ADJUSTED
7. BOMBING ALTITIJDE.............................. COMPUTED
8. DISC SPEED AND TRAIL IN
   BOMBSIGHT .... CHECKED
9. AB COMPUTER COMPLETELY
   SET UP .... CHECKED
10. BOMBING INTERVALOMETER
    SETTINGS... CHECKED
11. CAMERA INTERVALOMETER
    SETTINGS... CHECKED
12. CAMERA DOORS.................................... OPEN

BEFORE BOMBING RUN

1. BOMB BAY DOORS................................. OPEN
2. BOMBSIGHT STABILIZER....................... LEVEL
3. PROPER RACK SELECTOR
   SWITCHES .... ON
4. RELEASE HANDLE
   (OLD TYPE AIRCRAFT) .... SELECT
5. DRIFT AND DROPPING ANGLE .... PRE-SET

BEFORE LANDING

1. SWITCHES IN BOMBARDIER
   COMPARTMENT .... OFF
2. BOMBSIGHT.. POST-FLIGHTED
3. TURRETS AND GUNS............................. STOWED
4. GUNS, TURRETS, AND GUNSIGHT
   SWITCHES .... OFF
5. BOMBING EQUIPMENT
   MALFUNCTION REPORT .... COMPLETE
6. INTELLIGENCE REPORT........................ COMPLETE

It would be more than tragic to subject a bomber and its crew to the hazards of a mission, to consume irreplaceable time reaching the target, and then to discover that a malfunction prevents the successful accomplishment of that mission. You must avoid any such disastrous cancellation of a mission in the air that might have been prevented on the ground. The need for accurate preflighting of equipment, therefore, is only slightly less obvious than the need for accurate bombing procedure.

Crew Briefing

The purpose of briefing is to present to all crews, prior to takeoff, the maximum amount of reliable information pertinent to a mission. This information is given so that the crews can make their way along a designated route, correctly identify and bomb the target, and return safely by a prearranged plan.

The commanding officer announces the mission and shows the importance of the target in the plan of battle. The operations officer outlines the route out and return. He designates the units participating and types of formation to be flown, announces full time schedules, and issues landing instructions. He specifies the rendezvous points and IP; axis, altitude, and airspeed of attack; and operational data about the target and aiming point. Information is also provided on bomb loadings, fusing, fuel, ammunition, supply, special tactics, weather, and communications.

The intelligence officer describes the objective and covers details of the **alternate target** and **target of last resort**. He outlines the known enemy defenses and tactics, including AA batteries, fighter opposition, balloon barrages, dummies, and camouflage. All **friendly information** (convoys, balloon barrages, fighters, restricted areas, ground troops) is given.

The intelligence officer then reminds the crews of what to look for en route. He gives warnings and reminders on procedures in the event of forced landings in enemy territory.

The navigation officer gives a time tick. Then, announcement is made of further special briefing of pilots, bombardiers, navigators, and other crew members.

Special Bombardier Briefings

Special bombardier briefings are held to acquaint the bombardier with those facts about a mission which are particularly applicable to his job.

Despite extraordinary combat damage to the front of this B-17G of the 398th Bomb Group, sustained during a combat mission in 1944, the aircraft managed to reach home base, although the bombardier was killed. (USAAF)

The information is presented in a concise manner and covers all details of the mission from the IP to the target. Each bombardier is given a target folder, bombing tables, computers, stopwatch, and all other available bombing aids. The staff bombardier is usually in charge of these briefings.

The following information is presented:

Target identification. This covers the most prominent check points which aid in identifying the IP, those along the axis of attack, and those which bracket the target. The officer in charge of the briefing uses all available references to point out and emphasize landmarks and recognition features in the target area.

Approximate ETA over IP and distance from IP to target.

Type of sighting. The lead airplane may sight for both course and range, while wing airplanes release upon a signal from the leader or by visual recognition of lead airplane's release. Or the lead airplane may sight for both course and range and wing airplanes for range only. Or airplanes may make individual runs, as is the case in night operations.

Type of release and intervalometer settings.

Plan for evasive action if such action is to be used on the mission. Altitude and airspeed for bombing run.

Meteorological report. This includes direction and speed of winds at flight level and aloft of the target, surface winds at the target, predicted target temperature and temperatures aloft, mean temperature, and the target pressure altitude.

[. . .]

TARGET IDENTIFICATION CHECKLIST

When you have studied all your material and are ready to select your check points, use a checklist adapted to the theater of operations and the type of mission. The following checklist is general, but you can adapt it to your particular circumstances:

Target Area and Target

What is the general shape of the target?

What is its most outstanding visible feature?

How does it appear from different headings?

What combination of features encloses or boxes the target?

What lies in front of the target to provide the best check points if the target is obscured?

What secondary check points can you use if your main ones are obscured?

Will the shadows on the photographs be the same when you are over the target? At what time of day were they taken?

Terrain Identification

Since terrain features provide your check points, you must also check the completeness of your information about those you expect to encounter.

Will you encounter tidal water, and if so, what will be the effect of high or low tide on the terrain?

What are the distinguishing characteristics of the rivers in the region?

Can a canal be mistaken for a railroad? Is it likely to be camouflaged in part with netting?

What lakes or reservoirs are there, and what distinguishing shapes set them off from others in the region?

Do railroads funnel in toward target? If not, what other patterns do they make or form parts of?

What highways are near the target and what identifying features, such as clover-leaf overpasses or underpasses, do they have?

Are there any bridges sufficiently prominent to help identify the target?

Is the built-up area around the target dense, and if so, what characteristic design do its streets and squares form?

Is the built-up area sparsely settled?

If there is a smoke screen, can you tell where your target is from check points around the edges of the area?

Are there distinctively shaped patches of woods which cannot be confused with others nearby?

Have woods been confirmed by recent photos, or may the enemy have cut them, thus changing their shape?

What kinds of trees compose the woods—scrub, evergreen, deciduous?

Are there any city parks or other wooded sections in the built-up areas?

Are there any notable color differences in the terrain, such as the scars of road building?

Is there any construction of buildings, canals, railroads?

Are there such features as steep cliffs, which may cast shadows visible from your altitude?

Summary

What are the 5 main check points on any course, lying between 30 miles and 7 miles from the target?

What are the 5 main check points on any course, lying between 7 miles and 1 mile from the target?

What are the 5 main check points on any course, within 1 mile of the target?

In case the target is obscured and you have to use offset bombing, what points on the near side of the target can you use to synchronize on? How will you check on whether or not you are on course?

You must have a clear-cut impression of what you intend to look for in the target area from the air.

PREPARING TARGET FOLDER

When you have completed your analysis of all the available target material pertinent to your mission, select what will be most useful to you during the actual flight. Obviously, this will be the clearest and most recent coverage of the route just prior to the IP and the route into the target area. Don't burden yourself with excess material. Try to keep it to a minimum but select the best.

See that all your charts are clearly marked. A chart is meant to be used, marked on, and improved. Draw your course to the IP and your course from the IP to the target and circle your check points. Use pencils of different colors to differentiate between check points. It is advisable to overlay the 5° funnel (BIF 8-10-3) on your chart or to draw in some similar aid for the bombing approach.

All of the check points you find by study probably appear on your target charts. If you have found additional ones or have gathered other information that you may want quickly during flight, mark your chart accordingly.

Briefing provides you with other essential information. Camouflage, for instance, is not shown on navigational or target charts. If you have been told of camouflaged installations, mark them down.

Remember that a mission may or may not be planned to approach on one of the several headings for which you have perspectives. However, with 5 or 6 perspectives, each looking at the target from a different angle, you can easily interpolate a useful rough view for your actual approach.

When you have selected and marked the material you want, insert it in the target folder in the order in which you intend to use it. First, you should have an approach chart on which your route from the IP to target is outlined. Then come your target charts and perspectives and large scale charts. Insert photographs where they are most useful. You can put oblique photos, for instance, in the same leaf with the corresponding perspectives. Or, if you prefer, you can arrange all photographs in subsequent leaves. The important thing is to have an arrangement of material which lets you read your charts and photos quickly and without confusion.

If your target charts and perspectives are on separate sheets, put them into your target folder in such a way that you look quickly from one to the other. If they are on a single sheet, fold it so that only the sections which pertain to your selected bombing approach show.

Insert all maps and photographs into the leaves in such a way that you will read them **in the same direction**, the line of flight always being from bottom to top. **This is important**.

USING THE TARGET FOLDER

If you have prepared yourself, your charts, and your folder correctly, you begin your mission with a background of detailed information. In addition, you have a clear, simplified picture of the general pattern and important features of your target area. When you are in the air, dismiss from your mind all the small details of the chart. Concentrate on the prominent features you have chosen to guide you.

While it is far better to have four or five salient points in mind than a hazy idea of twenty, remember that any check point is of value to you when the main ones are hidden or you find yourself off course. Remember that the ground doesn't look exactly like the photographs you study. From your position in the airplane, you probably see many times the area covered by any one photograph. The photo does not show you colors, although, these appear on the terrain. It may have been taken from a heading, altitude, or angle which does not correspond to the actual flight of the airplane.

Don't be confused by these seeming discrepancies between study and practice. Your check points, or their alternatives, are there. By constant practice and observation whenever you are in flight you can train your eyes to recognize landmarks on the ground from all altitudes and angles.

[. . .]

TRAIN BOMBING

Train bombing gives you the best possible chance of partially or totally destroying your target. It consists of dropping an evenly spaced series of bombs across the target. The intervalometer controls the spacing of bombs in the train.

In releasing a train of bombs, you should release the first bomb to hit short of the target a distance equal to half the length of the train. Thus, you attempt to place the middle bomb of the train on the target's center. This makes it most likely that at least one or more bombs will hit the target in range.

To find the distance in mils that your first bomb must hit short of the target:

1. Find length of train of bombs by multiplying number of bombs minus 1 by interval in feet between successive bombs.
2. Find distance short, in feet, by dividing length of train by 2.
3. Convert the resulting distance in feet to distance in mils by multiplying it by 1000/BA.

The following equation summarizes these calculations:

$$\text{Mils short} = \frac{500 \,(\text{Number of bombs} -1) \times \text{Interval in feet}}{\text{Bombing Altitude}}$$

You can place the first bomb of your train the proper distance short of the target by decreasing trail, decreasing DS, or by selecting an aiming point the proper distance short of the target.

You can easily decrease the trail setting but, unless your bombsight has a trail spotting device, this may result in an appreciable error in crosstrail.

To find the proper amount to decrease DS:

1. Determine approximate mil value of 1 rpm decrease in DS. To find it, double the GS you expect to have over the target and divide that figure by 100.
2. Determine number of rpm to decrease DS. You do this by dividing mil value per rpm into number of mils needed to cause first bomb to hit half train length short of target.

If a definite object, such as a road or building, is on your axis of attack and the proper distance short of the center of your target, you can use it as the aiming point. This will place the mean point of impact (MPI) of your train of bombs on the target's center without requiring you to decrease trail or DS.

When using the intervalometer:

1. Place train-select switch at TRAIN at least 1 minute prior to release.
2. Set counter knob pointer at number of bombs desired in train. If releasing in train all the bombs on the racks, set pointer at a number greater than your entire load to make sure you drop them all.
3. Set GS you expect to have over target opposite desired bomb spacing.

When your indices meet, check to see if intervalometer is working properly. If a malfunction occurs and all bombs have not been released, salvo remainder or change train-select switch to SELECT and toggle them as fast as possible.

[. . .]

FORMATION BOMBING

Early formation bombing consisted of bombing in elements of 3 airplanes. As enemy opposition has increased, formations have been enlarged to include 6, 12, 18, and 21 airplanes. These larger formations are employed to provide heavier fire power when deep penetrations are made into areas which are heavily defended.

Two methods of bombing are normally used by formations of airplanes: individual range bombing and pattern bombing.

In individual range bombing, all airplanes in the formation carry bombsights. The leader sights for range and deflection and the wing bombardiers' sight for range only.

Because the bombing platform in a wing airplane is unstable while the airplane is trying to maintain formation, individual range bombing has not been especially effective. It has resulted in patterns being scattered and inaccurate with bombs falling before and behind the target.

In pattern bombing, the lead bombardier sights for both course and range and the wing bombardiers drop their bombs on the leader, either when they sight the lead airplane's bombs being released, or upon a prearranged signal.

Pattern bombing with dependable lead bombardiers is yielding better results today. By this method more bombs are being placed in the target area in a more compact pattern. Best bombing patterns are made by groups which fly the best formations. Good formation flying and quick release on the leader are the keys to effective pattern bombing.

Good formation bombing gives you the desired pattern in **width**. The intervalometer in the airplane is designed to give you the desired pattern in **length**. Remember, when you release bombs on the leader you must have a dependable means of identifying his bombs.

Although the practical maximum of airplanes in a formation which bombs off the leader has not been agreed upon, formations of from 6 to 12 airplanes have proven successful and are widely used.

HIGH ALTITUDE BOMBING

Bombing which is done from an altitude of 15,000 feet and above is commonly called high altitude bombing. However, that does not imply bombing from the maximum or service ceiling of your airplane. The bombing altitude must be chosen to permit successful destruction of the target without too great a loss in men and equipment.

If you can bomb a target successfully from 15,000 feet without unduly jeopardizing the safety of your crew and airplane, do not bomb from a higher altitude. You will reduce accuracy by doing so and you may have to go back a second time to finish your job. Effective bombing results demand your utmost in technical skill and accuracy. They also demand painstaking study of the target and target area. With the aid of maps, photos, and target guides, you must fix a picture of the target so firmly in your mind that you can bomb successfully even when only a part of the target area is visible.

Bombing Approach

Before trying to locate the IP itself, identify the larger landmarks and terrain features near it. The IP is easier to find if you first locate the area surrounding it.

Work with the navigator to locate the IP by pinpointing the most prominent features. But don't rely entirely on him to find your check points for you. If you can't locate the IP with certainty but have identified several check points around it you are justified in making your turn on the briefed axis of attack. Don't go fishtailing all over the sky trying to find a dot on the map from 15,000 feet or higher.

Make sure you turn on the correct heading and hold it until you have identified the check points to the left and right of the course, then to the left and right of the target. Then narrow down your vision and your course.

Don't look too far ahead for the target. Keep yourself oriented on check points. Well chosen check points help you time your bombing run and establish an approximate course and range synchronization before the target itself is in sight.

Because it's hard to tell by check points how far you are from the target and how long it will take to get there, learn to use the sighting angle to make these estimates. It is your most reliable means. Use the graph which has been prepared to give you the distance to the target at any sighting angle and at your bombing altitude. Use your predetermined groundspeed to estimate the time it will take to cover that distance.

If the target is obscured by smoke from previous bombs or by a smoke screen, place the crosshairs and synchronize on a check point along the axis of attack as close to the target as possible. Then displace the crosshairs to the approximate location of the target. By using the computer grid or some similar device, you can do offset aiming with reasonable accuracy.

During the bombing approach the airplane is yours. You are responsible for doing or directing the evasive action. Speak up. Let the crew know what you need and when you need it.

Bombing Run

You must be ready for flak and rough air. Although the gyro has been leveled the bubbles may shift erratically. **This does not necessarily mean that the gyro is tumbling**.

On a bombing run of average length, level your gyro bubbles once and the gyro will maintain the level you establish. On a long bombing run, minor leveling adjustments may be necessary. Do not cage and

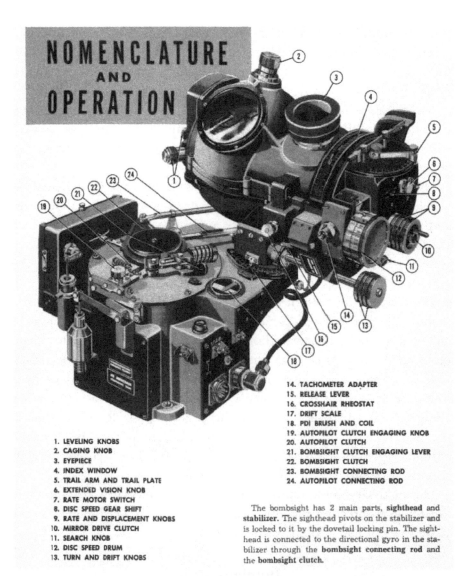

NOMENCLATURE AND OPERATION

1. LEVELING KNOBS
2. CAGING KNOB
3. EYEPIECE
4. INDEX WINDOW
5. TRAIL ARM AND TRAIL PLATE
6. EXTENDED VISION KNOB
7. RATE MOTOR SWITCH
8. DISC SPEED GEAR SHIFT
9. RATE AND DISPLACEMENT KNOBS
10. MIRROR DRIVE CLUTCH
11. SEARCH KNOB
12. DISC SPEED DRUM
13. TURN AND DRIFT KNOBS

14. TACHOMETER ADAPTER
15. RELEASE LEVER
16. CROSSHAIR RHEOSTAT
17. DRIFT SCALE
18. PDI BRUSH AND COIL
19. AUTOPILOT CLUTCH ENGAGING KNOB
20. AUTOPILOT CLUTCH
21. BOMBSIGHT CLUTCH ENGAGING LEVER
22. BOMBSIGHT CLUTCH
23. BOMBSIGHT CONNECTING ROD
24. AUTOPILOT CONNECTING ROD

The bombsight has 2 main parts, **sighthead** and stabilizer. The sighthead pivots on the stabilizer and is locked to it by the dovetail locking pin. The sighthead is connected to the directional gyro in the stabilizer through the **bombsight connecting rod** and the **bombsight clutch.**

uncage the gyro on the bombing run as a substitute for good leveling. **The caging knob is for caging the gyro. It is not a leveling knob**.

If you find the bombing run too short, or if weather or man-made conditions obscure the target, you may have to make a new bombing approach. Decide on your new plan of action quickly. Let the pilot know what the conditions are. He not only will listen but will usually act promptly on your advice.

A bombing run that is too short may ruin the whole show. If you don't do the job right the first time you will probably have to go back and the enemy will be ready and waiting. If you miss the IP, you may have to hurry your procedure to the detriment of your accuracy. A well timed run with systematic procedure and undivided concentration is your best bet for efficient bombing.

Hints

Dress warmly, but not tightly.

Always use the oxygen mask microphone, making sure the connecting plugs fit firmly.

Use whatever de-icing facilities are available, such as heating pads, air blasts, ventilators, and heating fans, to remove ice from the inside of the Plexiglas nose.

To minimize condensation and frosting on the bombsight eyepiece and telescope window, wipe them with a lint-free cloth or remove them. Make use of your bombsight heating covers.

At low temperatures, before reaching the IP check to see if the optics are fogging. If they are, remove the telescope window and insert the beater tube. If you notice fogging in sufficient time before you need to use the bombsight, you can clear the condensation this way.

Always discuss each bombing mission with the pilot before takeoff. The better you both understand in advance what each of you is going to do, the less likelihood there is of a misunderstanding.

Utilize all the aid that your navigator can give you.

Always follow the briefed course to avoid colliding with other airplanes.

If you are deputy lead bombardier, always be prepared to take over if something happens to the lead airplane.

Raise and lock your release lever before you start the bombing run. On the bombing run you are apt to overlook it.

When bombing with the use of POI, be sure your pilot understands what you are doing. Always make clear to him what you want him to do. Give him a chance to follow your corrections.

The optics blacks out if a steep bank is made. Your gyro has not necessarily tumbled. The optics returns to normal when the airplane levels out, and the eyepiece is again above the telescope.

When a smoke screen obscures the target, attack down the ground wind if possible. Frequently you can see between the smoke furrows and locate check points which you can use for offset bombing.

When many groups attack one target, most of them find it obscured by bombfall smoke. Be well prepared to do offset bombing when this happens. Never aim at top of smoke columns.

In selecting the proper axis of attack for a bombing run consider: position of sun; selection of a suitable IP; shape of target; wind direction and speed; AA fire around target.

MEDIUM ALTITUDE BOMBING

The operation of the bombsight and the general bombing problem at medium altitudes are essentially the same as at high altitudes. However, there are a few differences:

Medium bombardment is employed principally to neutralize enemy airfields and to cut his lines of communication. Because of limited operational range, medium bombardment is used in strategic bombing only to supplement heavy bombardment

Targets most commonly selected for medium bombardment are marshaling yards, railroad and highway bridges, and airfield installations. When it is used in direct support of ground forces, troop concentrations and ammunition and supply dumps also become objectives. In the bombing of bridges or any other rectangular targets, it has been found that an axis of attack at an angle of 45° to 90° with the target's longitudinal axis offers the best opportunity for a direct hit.

Formations

Careful analysis of past bombing records of medium and heavy bombardment reveals that bombing accuracy definitely increases as bombing formations decrease in size. The amount of enemy air opposition expected usually dictates the type of formation used for bombing. However, for targets such as those encountered in medium bombardment it is believed that the most effective and accurate method of attack is by flights of 6 airplanes so spaced as to give the desired pattern.

In each flight of 6 airplanes the lead bombardier sights for range and deflection while the wing bombardiers drop on the leader. Medium altitude missions are usually carried out with pre-set data subject only to minor corrections. That is because runs are shorter and the object is to get over the target and out again in the shortest possible time. However, bombing accuracy should not be sacrificed in the attempt to avoid flak.

Teamwork is of paramount importance because many medium bombardment airplanes are not as yet equipped with autopilots. Evasive action with short bombing runs is almost indispensable at medium altitudes because of the intensity of AA fire by automatic weapons and the greater degree of accuracy obtained by heavy guns. The pilot must develop a high degree of skill in following the PDI. He must know what to expect from the bombardier. When he does, he can fly the airplane in such a way to provide maximum help for the bombardier on the bombing run.

MINIMUM ALTITUDE BOMBING

Minimum altitude bombing has been and is being carried on in Pacific theaters with a high degree of success against targets both on land and at sea. Predetermined computations are pre-set into the bombsights. Tactics employed in such attacks vary with the target.

Minimum altitude bombing against shipping or pinpoint targets may employ a single airplane or a coordinated attack of two or more airplanes, depending upon expected opposition. The practice is to drop 3 bombs, spaced to bracket the target. The second bomb should be a direct hit.

Minimum altitude bombing is often accomplished from a line-abreast formation (for maximum simultaneous strafing power) of as many airplanes as are necessary to cover the target area. Bomb fuses used are such that explosion does not occur until the airplane is a safe distance away. The bombs can be dropped in train or toggled out at opportune intervals, depending upon the size and type of target. With some types of bombs, it is often necessary for the bomber to increase altitude slightly before releasing them. This makes the bomber more vulnerable to enemy fire from automatic weapons.

The **advantages** of this method of bombing are:

Element of surprise.

Good visibility of target at time of release.

Reduced exposure to heavy ground artillery.

Photographic possibilities.

Bombs fall from Martin B-26 Marauders targeting a railroad bridge across the Moselle river at Trier-Pfalzel, Rhineland-Palatinate, Germany, in December 1944. (NARA/LOC)

The bomber can also strafe, a form of attack which restricts enemy ground observation.

Short approaches are possible and evasive tactics can be used until almost al bomb release point.

The **disadvantages** are;

The bomber is within range of automatic ground weapons and flak towers.

Airplanes flying line–abreast formation cannot veer much from course and must travel a given path.

Hints

When meeting fire from automatic weapons:

Fly straight through area as rapidly as possible.

Take advantage of terrain features which will confuse the gunners, making it difficult for them to distinguish between airplane and background.

Try to lay out a course in advance, or at the last moment if necessary, which will make the enemy gunners' brief problem as difficult as possible.

You can often surprise the enemy by:

Taking advantage of masking characteristics of terrain, such as mountain peaks, craters, jungle growth.

Varying axis of attack. There are certain desirable approaches to every defended area. Because they are best, the defense is usually set up with these in mind. If you can avoid these approaches, you achieve a certain amount of surprise.

Use speed, terrain, and weather to full advantage.

CHAPTER 4

Navigator and Radio Operator

Although navigators and radio operators typically had less of the high-profile status of pilots and bombardiers, they were both critical to the outcome of the bomber mission—there was no dead wood carried in a bomber crew. The navigator's job was particularly central, as he was responsible for guiding the aircraft to and from its final destination, doing so by a complicated mix of methods, summarized in the first manual extract below. His job was intellectually demanding. Throughout the mission his eyes would be glued to maps, charts, instruments, ground features, data sheets, weather cards, flight plans, and much other paraphernalia, constantly updating flight information and feeding corrections and updates to the pilot. The path to the target would have been planned out in detail hours before the operation began, often in the early hours of the morning—mental stamina was a key requirement of a navigator. But he also needed fighting spirit. He would often be required to man guns and fire them professionally, or perform all manner of manual duties, such as freeing bombs stuck in their bomb racks.

The following B-24 pilot manual capably summarizes the roles of both navigator and radio operator and explains how they integrated their actions with those in the cockpit. What is interesting is the contrast between the respect for the navigator but the air of suspicion about the radio operator's capabilities and training. Radio operators were responsible for the equipment and procedures of combat communications. They had to understood both the abstract principles of radio communications and the technical specifics of the radio sets and electronic navigation instruments on board. On a B-17, for example, the radio operator would oversee the SCR-274-N Command Radio, used for communications with proximate in-flight aircraft and approaching ground stations; the long-range SCR-287-A Liaison Radio, capable of voice and Morse communications; the SCR-522-A

VHF Command Radio for communications with a range of about 150 miles (241 km); and the SCR-269-G Radio Compass, used in tandem with on-ground radio beacons for direction finding. Like the navigators, the radiomen were also trained as gunners—everyone on board was ultimately a combatant.

From *Pilot Training Manual for the B-24 Liberator* (1945)

NAVIGATOR

The navigator's job is to direct your flight from departure to destination and return. He must know the exact position of the airplane at all times. In order for you to understand fully how best to get most reliable service from your navigator, you must know as much about his job as possible.

Navigation is the art of determining geographic positions by means of (a) pilotage, (b) dead reckoning, (c) radio, or (d) celestial navigation, or any combination of these 4 methods. By any one or combination of methods the navigator determines the position of the airplane in relation to the earth.

Pilotage

Pilotage is the method of determining the airplane's position by visual reference to the ground. The importance of accurate pilotage cannot be overstressed. In combat navigation, all bombing targets are approached by pilotage, and in many theaters the route is maintained by pilotage. This requires not merely the vicinity type, but pin-point pilotage. The exact position of the airplane must be known not within 5 miles, but within ¼ of a mile.

The navigator does this by constant reference to groundspeeds, the ground, and to his maps and charts. ETAs are established for points ahead. During the mission, as long as he can maintain visual contact with the ground, the navigator can establish these pin-point positions so that the exact track of the airplane will be known when the mission is completed.

Dead Reckoning

Dead reckoning is the basis of all other types of navigation. For instance, if the navigator is doing pilotage, and computes ETAs for points ahead, he is using dead reckoning.

Dead reckoning determines the position of the airplane at any given time by keeping an account of the track and distance flown over the earth's surface from the point of departure or the last known position.

Dead reckoning can be subdivided into two classes:

1. **Dead reckoning based on a series of known positions.** For example, you, as pilot, start on a mission at 25,000 feet. For the first hour your navigator keeps track by pilotage, at the same time recording the heading and airspeed which you are holding. According to plan at the end of the first hour the airplane goes above the clouds, thus losing contact with the ground. By means of dead reckoning from his last pilotage point, the navigator is able to tell the position of the aircraft at any time. The first hour's travel has given him the wind prevalent at the altitude, and the track and groundspeed being made. By computing track and distance from the last pilotage point, he can always tell the position of the airplane. When your airplane comes out of the clouds near the target, the navigator will have a very close approximation of his exact position and will be able to pick up pilotage points very quickly.

2. **Dead reckoning as a result of visual references other than pilotage.** When flying over water, desert, or barren land, where no reliable pilotage points are available, very accurate DR navigation still can be performed. By means of the drift meter the navigator is able to determine drift, the angle between the heading of the aircraft and the track of the aircraft over the ground. The true heading of the aircraft is obtained by application of compass error to the compass reading. The true heading plus or minus the drift (as read on the drift meter) gives the track of the airplane. At a constant airspeed, drift on 2 or more headings will give the navigator information necessary to obtain the wind by use of his computer. Groundspeed is computed easily once the wind, heading, and airspeed are known. So by constant recording of true heading, true airspeed, drift, and groundspeed, the navigator is able to determine accurately the position of the aircraft at any given time. For greatest accuracy, constant courses and airspeeds must be maintained by the pilot. If course or airspeed is changed, notify the navigator so he can record these changes.

Radio

Radio navigation makes use of various radio aids to determine position. The development of many new radio devices has increased the use of radio in combat zones. However, the ease with which radio aids can be jammed, or bent, limits the use of radio to that of a check on DR and pilotage. The navigator, in conjunction with the radioman, is responsible for all radio procedures, approaches, etc., that are in effect in the theater.

Celestial

Celestial navigation is the science of determining position by reference to 2 or more celestial bodies. The navigator uses a sextant accurate time and numerous tables to obtain what he calls a line of position. Actually, this line is part of a circle on which the altitude of the particular body is constant for that instant of time.

An intersection of 2 or more of these lines gives the navigator a fix. These fixes can be relied on as being accurate within approximately 10 miles. The reason for inaccuracy is the instability of the airplane as it moves through space, causing acceleration of the sextant bubble (a level denoting the horizontal). Because of this acceleration, the navigator takes observations over a period of time so that the acceleration error will cancel out to some extent. If the navigator tells the pilot when he wishes to take an observation, extremely careful flying on the part of the pilot during the few minutes it takes to make the observations will result in much greater accuracy. Generally speaking, the only celestial navigation used by a combat crew is during the delivering flight to the theater. But in all cases celestial navigation is used as a check on dead reckoning and pilotage except where celestial is the only method available, such as on long over-water flights, etc.

Instrument Calibration

Instrument calibration is an important duty of the navigator. All navigation depends directly on the accuracy of his instruments. Correct calibration requires close cooperation and extremely careful flying by the pilot. Instruments to be calibrated include the altimeter, all compasses, airspeed

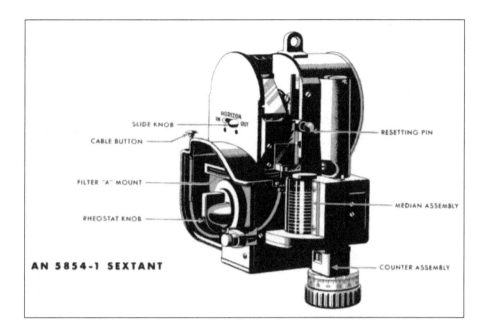

SLIDE KNOB

HORIZON IN OUT

RESETTING PIN

CABLE BUTTON

FILTER "A" MOUNT

MEDIAN ASSEMBLY

RHEOSTAT KNOB

AN 5854-1 SEXTANT

COUNTER ASSEMBLY

indicators, alignment of the astrocompass, astrograph, and drift meter, and checks on the navigator's sextant and watch.

Pilot-Navigator Preflight Planning

1. Pilot and navigator must study flight plan of the route to be flown and select alternate airports.
2. Study the weather **with** the navigator. Know what weather you are likely to encounter. Decide what action is to be taken. Know the weather conditions at the alternate airports.
3. Inform your navigator of what airspeed and altitude you wish to fly so that he can prepare his flight plan.
4. Learn what type of navigation the navigator intends to use: pilotage, dead reckoning, radio, celestial, or a combination of all methods.
5. Determine check points; plan to make radio fixes.
6. Work out an effective communication method with your navigator to be used in flight.
7. Synchronize your watch with your navigator's.

Pilot–Navigator in Flight

1. **Constant course**—For accurate navigation you, the pilot, must fly a constant course. The navigator has many computations and notations to make in his log. Constantly changing course makes his job more difficult. A good navigator is supposed to be able to follow the pilot, but he cannot be taking compass readings all the time.

2. **Constant airspeed** must be held as nearly as possible. This is as important to the navigator as is a constant course in determining position.

3. **Precision flying** by the pilot greatly affects the accuracy of the navigator's instrument readings, particularly celestial readings. A slight error in celestial reading can cause considerable error in determining positions. You can help the navigator by providing as steady a platform as possible from which he can take readings. The navigator should notify you when he intends to take readings so that the airplane can be leveled off and flown as smoothly as possible preferably by using the automatic pilot. Do not allow your navigator to be disturbed while he is taking celestial readings.

4. **Notify the navigator in advance of any change in flight** such as change in altitude, course, or airspeed. If change in flight plan is to be made, consult the navigator. Talk over the proposed change so that he can plan the flight and advise you concerning it.

5. In the event there is doubt as to the position of the airplane, pilot and navigator should work together, refer to the navigator's flight log, talk the problem over and decide together the best course of action to take.

6. Check your compasses at intervals with those of the navigator, noting any deviation.

7. Require your navigator to give position reports at regular intervals.

8. You are ultimately responsible for getting the airplane to its destination. Therefore, it is your duty to know your position at all times.

9. Encourage your navigator to use as many of the methods of navigation as possible as a means of double-checking and for practice.

Post-flight Critique

After every flight get together with the navigator and discuss the flight and compare notes. Go over the navigator's log. If there have been serious navigational errors, discuss them with the navigator and determine their cause. If the navigator has been at fault, caution him that it is his job to see that the same mistake does not occur again. If the error has been caused by faulty instruments, see that they are corrected before another navigation mission is attempted. If your flying has contributed to the inaccuracy of the navigation, try to fly a better course the next mission.

Miscellaneous Duties

The navigator's primary duty is navigating your airplane with a high degree of accuracy. But as a member of the team, he must also have a general knowledge of the entire operation of the airplane.

He has a .50-cal. machine gun at his station, and he must be able to use it skillfully and to service it in emergencies.

He must be familiar with the oxygen system, know how to operate the turrets, radio equipment, and fuel transfer system.

He must know the location of all fuses and spare fuses, lights and spare lights, affecting navigation.

He must be familiar with emergency procedures, such as the manual operation of landing gear, bomb bay doors, and flaps, and the proper procedures for crash landings, ditching, bailout, etc.

[. . .]

THE RADIO OPERATOR

There is a lot of radio equipment in today's B-24s. There is one special man who is supposed to know all there is to know about this equipment. Sometimes he does but often he doesn't. His deficiencies often do not become apparent until the crew is in the combat zone, when it is too late. Too often the lives of pilots and crew are lost because the radio operator has accepted his responsibility indifferently.

Radio is a subject that cannot be learned in a day. It cannot be mastered in 6 weeks, but sufficient knowledge can be imparted to the

A B-24 *Liberator* of the 7th Bomb Group attacks a bridge of the Moulmein–Ye rail line in Burma on January 27, 1945. Rivers and rail lines provided invaluable navigational guides. (NARA)

radio man during his period of training in the United States providing he is willing to study.

It is imperative that you check your radio operator's ability to handle his job before taking him overseas as part of your crew. To do this you may have to check the various instructor departments to find out any weakness in the radio operator's training and proficiency and to aid the instructors in overcoming such weaknesses.

Training in the various phases of the heavy bomber program is designed to fit each member of the crew for the handling of his jobs. The radio operator will be required to:

1. Render position reports every 30 minutes.
2. Assist the navigator in taking fixes.

3. Keep the liaison and command sets properly tuned and in good operating order.
4. Understand from an operational point of view:
   (a) Instrument landing
   (b) IFF
   (c) VHF
   and other navigational aids equipment in your airplane.
5. Maintain a log.

In addition to being radio operator, the radio man is also a gunner. During periods of combat, he will be required to leave his watch at the radio and take up his guns. He is often required to learn photography. Some of the best pictures taken in the Southwest Pacific were taken by radio operators. The radio operator who cannot perform his job properly may be the weakest member of your crew. And the crew is no stronger than its weakest member.

Weatherbirds

While the bulk of USAAF bombers were committed to combat operations, thousands of the aircraft were purposed for non-combat operations that nonetheless carried genuine dangers. One such mission was that conducted by "weatherbird" B-17s, which made weather reconnaissance sorties over the Atlantic. These were true endurance missions, often lasting 14–15 hours through some of the worst Atlantic weather systems. Aircraft would sometimes never return, vanishing without trace or record over the vast ocean. The following account of one such operation was written by Major Arthur Gordon in May 1944. We can note the critical importance of the navigator and radio operator to these missions:

> The mission actually begins several hours before take-off time with the briefing. It's not very elaborate: a forecast of weather conditions likely to be encountered, a shipping situation summary giving position of convoys that may be met, the radio call signals of the day, and so forth. When the crew is at its home base a specially assigned intelligence officer conducts the briefing. If it has landed at another airdrome the unit commanding officer may give the briefing himself, having received the information by phone.

After briefing the crew disperses for food and as much sleep as the time of take-off will allow. At breakfast the atmosphere is completely relaxed, in sharp contrast to the tension before a combat mission. Officers and non-coms kid each other about alleged amatory exploits. The camaraderie persists as they drive out to the hardstand where the B-17 is waiting, with a stencilled row of miniature weathervanes on her nose, each symbolizing a successful weather flight, barely visible in the dim light.

Only the British meteorological officer is somewhat aloof. Not unfriendly but rather shy, as might be expected when a lone Briton finds himself in an air crew with seven uninhibited Americans. Tall and rather awkward, he pulls a British helmet down over his ears and crawls into the B-17 carrying a bag which contains his meteorological tables and a thermos bottle that almost certainly contains tea. He makes his way forward into the plexiglass nose of the bomber and draws a curtain behind him so that the light from the navigators table will not affect his vision. He sits up there on his little stool confronting his instruments:

An aneroid barometer that records air pressure in millibars, a cyclometer which consists of two thermometers, one air and the other wet-bulb, a pressure altimeter and an air speed indicator. Every fifty miles through the darkness of the night—and the daylight hours, too—like some high priest of weather, he will perform the ritual to which the whole mission is dedicated. What he observes in the way of temperature changes, wind veers and cloud formations, all details of vapor trails, icing conditions, warm and cold fronts, is carefully recorded.

Behind the "met" officer sits the navigator. He is the next most important man of the team. He has secret equipment to aid him in plotting his position while the Fortress is fairly near land, but for most of the distance he has to rely on dead reckoning and celestial navigation.

The main worry of the pilot and copilot is getting the big ship off the ground. Once they have a few hundred feet of altitude they can relax. But beforehand they check each engine carefully. If any of the engines seems to be running rough they will not risk a takeoff. An alternate Fortress is always standing by. Rather than take chances they will transfer to it.

In the radio room, social center of the ship, the non-coms are gathered for the take-off: engineer, radio-men, ball-turret and waist gunners. On the floors are stacked provisions looted from the mess to keep the crew from being hungry on the fifteen-hour trip: bread, butter, peanut butter, jam, self-heating soup, cheese, candy bars—hardly a balanced diet but a lot better than nothing.

Of these four men, the radio operator is probably busiest throughout the long trip. The waist and ball-turret gunners share the job of dropping smoke bombs to calculate drift. Sometimes they test their guns by shooting at the bombs.

Technical Sergeant Arthur L. Smith, the radio-operator and gunner of *Our Gang*, a B-17 Flying Fortress operating from England, orientates himself to his weapon before taking off on another mission over enemy territory, June 24, 1943. (Signal Corps Archive)

★★★

The following manual text is from Combat Crew Manual: XX Bomber Command APO 493 *(1944). It explains the principles and practices of combat navigation and radio operation, as applied specifically within the operational conditions of XX Bomber Command. During World War II, there were four bomber commands responsible for the strategic bombing campaign directed against Germany and Japan, each of the bomber commands residing within a specific Air Force command structure. The most well-studied historically is VIII Bomber Command within the Eighth Air Force, the vanguard bombing instrument against Germany between 1942 and 1945, flying mainly from air bases in the UK. IX Bomber Command, Ninth Air Force, at first covered the Mediterranean Theater of Operations (MTO), but in the summer of 1943 it was transferred to the UK to act as a tactical bombardment force to support the future Allied invasion of Normandy, being redesignated 9th Bombardment Division (Medium) in*

A B-29A Superfortress on operation in 1945; such aircraft had a combat range of more than 3,000 miles, hence they were ideally suited to Pacific missions. (USAAF)

August 1944 and 9th Air Division (Bombardment) in May 1945. XX Bomber Command, Twentieth Air Force, was activated in November 1943 for operations against Japan and Japanese-occupied territories in Southeast Asia, flying from bases in those parts of China not occupied by Japanese forces. Finally, XXI Bomber Command, also within the Twentieth Air Force, was another Japan-focused organization, flying B-29s out from the Mariana Islands on very-long-range missions against the Japanese homeland.

From *Combat Crew Manual: XX Bomber Command APO 493* (1944)

VI. COMBAT NAVIGATION

The requirement for first class navigation is extremely important in a Very Long Range bomber. The fundamental problem of getting to the target and back to base as prescribed in the field order is a long arduous, and difficult one in VLR airplanes and it is further complicated in Asiatic operations by difficult weather conditions, poorly charted terrain, and few aids to navigation. The most important phase of navigation develops from tactical operations, and you can't afford to be satisfied with mediocre results or efforts. You have to be right the first time. The necessary combat and flying odds against a successful mission are sufficient without adding further uncertainty from equipment trouble and lack of knowledge, technique, and cooperation.

A. CALIBRATION OF EQUIPMENT

The navigator's instruments are the source of his most important information and he must continually work against an increasing tendency that develops in the field to "get by" with instruments as they are. The compass, airspeed meter, and octant should get loving care and the most exact calibration. All instruments should be calibrated in accordance with XX Bomber Command Memorandum 55-12.

B. THE NAVIGATOR AND THE CREW

Aside from the proper working of your equipment and your individual proficiency, getting there and getting back requires the cooperation of all the crew members so good decisions can be made and all available information and techniques can be put to best use.

1. Navigator - Pilot.

Navigator-pilot cooperation is absolutely essential in combat navigation. Decisions should be mutual and completely in accord with the pilot's and your estimate of a situation. A pilot should have unquestioned confidence in his navigator's navigation decision and you should by deed and diligence deserve this confidence. The pilot should appreciate the importance of engendering and cultivating your confidence in yourself. You should teach your pilot how hard it is to take a shot in an unsteady airplane, how important it is to fly a good course, and how important it is to fly climbs and let-downs according to plan.

2. Navigator - Bombardier.

You can expect from the bombardier pilotage information, drift checks, ground speed, and wind direction and velocity. You can provide the bombardier with ground speed, wind direction and velocity, and target identification help.

3. Navigator - Radio Operator.

You can get from the radio operator QDMs, QTEs, QTFs [types of magnetic and direction-finding station bearing information], relative and true bearings from the radio compass, and sundry information the radio operator picks up by listening. You will give the radio operator times at which necessary reports must be made.

4. Navigator - Radar Operator.

The radar operator can give you ground speed, wind direction and velocity, coastline landfalls, drift checks, and fixes according to azimuth and ground range. You can help the radar operator orient himself.

5. Navigator - Flight Engineer.

You and the flight engineer are the two people who integrate the two vastly important factors of: "How much gas have we?" and "How far do we have to go?" A fuel consumption expert remarked of B-29 navigators, "Analysis of flight logs to date shows that increased navigation proficiency will do much to reduce the variation in fuel consumption among airplanes on the same mission. This is a very lucrative source for improvement in overall efficiency and every possible means should be used to impress the navigator with the effect his errors have on the fuel consumed."

In the first raids on Japan some of the navigators were very impressed with the effect their errors had on the fuel consumed; they will not forget how close they came to not getting back: Some did not get back. Work with your flight engineer and learn the gas problem.

6. Navigator - Gunners.

You learn from the gunners important intelligence data of all kinds to record properly in your log.

C. STANDARD PROCEDURES

The procedures set forth here apply to lead and wing navigators alike. The distinction between lead and wing navigators is essentially one of responsibility. The lead navigator is responsible for getting the formation to the target and back as directed in the field order. Wing navigators, though handicapped by the difficulties encountered navigating on a wing, accomplish the same navigation that the lead navigator accomplishes. The only difference in navigation is one of method. Wing navigators do DR based on follow-the-pilot procedures.

1. Flight Plan.

It is considered good procedure to have at hand before a mission as many answers as possible concerning the proposed flight. The best aggregate of answers you can produce is a detailed flight plan based on the latest winds made out with the help of the flight engineer and pilot. No-wind flight plans in Asia do not depart very much from actual flight times except in the rare cases or extremely strong winds. When first hand information is limited a flight plan properly followed provides a good general basis on which to make decisions. You are required to make a flight plan for each mission.

2. Logbook.

A carefully made, accurate log is the best testament to your procedure and technique. A navigator can not do everything required of him unless he has an orderly procedure--a good log is the basis of an orderly procedure. The log is also an official document--the record of the mission. It is subject to scrutiny and review by higher headquarters for many reasons included among which are: Investigation of an operational loss involving navigation difficulty, investigation of claims made by the airplane commander which involve questions of time and place, investigations of operational performance, and investigations concerning tactical performance. Navigation logs ere checked after every mission.

3. Navigation Procedure Based on DR.

Navigation itself is fundamentally dead reckoning: Time, direction, speed, distance, altitude, and wind are the basic elements. Your ability to navigate stems from your ability to dead reckon accurately. In this Command you will consider dead reckoning the principal method of navigation and practice it and its counterpart of follow-the-pilot with

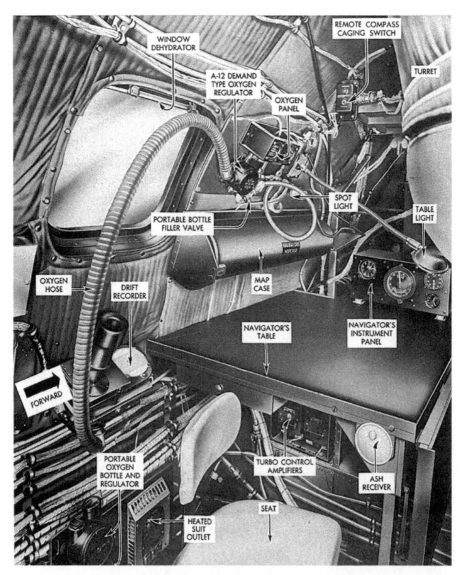

B-29 navigator's station

meticulous care at all times during a mission. If you dead-reckon well, the auxiliary methods of navigation and aids to navigation can be used to a much greater advantage. If you dead-reckon well and use all the information available along with old fashioned horse sense you won't be in trouble.

D. RADIO AND RADAR AIDS

Thus far radio navigation has not been developed to a high degree in the India-Burma and China Theaters where it is affected by weather, terrain, and great distances. You must, nevertheless, learn how to use it to the best advantage close-in because in many cases it's the only way you will find your field. You must learn how to ask for, evaluate, and use a QDM, a QTE, and a QTF. You must learn how to interpret single radio LOP's [line of position] which you can obtain from your radio compass. In addition to D/F and homers there are some radio ranges and YJ beacons. Learning to use these aids during bad weather when you need them most requires a great deal of attention and technique. You must be able to use them. Radar is an aid which you carry with you in the airplane and it is of tremendous value over and near coasts and over relatively flat areas where rivers and modern towns may be found. Rader does not prove to be much of an aid over mountainous area but with practice it can be used most of the time over land to obtain ground speed and drift. Very often radar provides the only information available. Learn how to use it in cooperation with your radar operator.

E. CELESTIAL NAVIGATION

Celestial navigation requires considerable equipment, accurate time, and a navigator with a high degree of training. It is not satisfactory unless the navigator practices constantly to maintain his technique. The principal of celestial navigation at night or day is without equal in theory. The procedure is comparatively simple; the resources are adequate, providing the sky is visible; it cannot be interfered with by the enemy; and the necessary equipment is carried entirely within the aircraft. In Asia celestial navigation has been hampered by weather from time to time, but on every mission, it has been used to advantage. As has been pointed out above, navigation aids are limited and because of that a Group Commander of a famous Heavy Group in China remarked "Celestial navigation in this Theater is at its zenith." It is up to you to practice celestial unceasingly in the air when your ground position is known so you will be familiar with and will have solved or compromised the many problems of combat celestial in a B-29. You will know then what to expect of yourself when you need a shot or a fix desperately. Celestial navigation, the highest form of your art, is stressed in this Command.

F. LANDFORMS. PILOTAGE AND CHARTS

Of all the theaters probably the least is known about terrain in yours. Use of maps and charts in the normal manner is not possible. If you are able to follow a course mile by mile on the ground often charts may be used for pilotage, but this is almost never the case. Charts of India and the "Hump" are reasonably good except for altitudes on the "Hump" and rivers which are at flood tide during the monsoon. Charts of inland China are to be used with caution as only the most prominent of land-forms and cities are reliable. Rivers are disproportionately charted and mischarted and terrain altitudes are off as much as five or six thousand feet in some areas. Except when near the coast (the China coast itself is not charted too well) the best policy is to DR on a master chart using radio, celestial, and radar to the best advantage and not to confuse yourself by trying to pinpoint the airplane by reference to the pilotage charts and ground. You must learn to know this wild country and to build up on your master mercator a file of accurate pilotage information as well as to help build up a fund of accurate information in your Group. Orientation from charts in coastal regions is not difficult either visually or by the use of radar.

G. WEATHER STUDY

Your knowledge of weather conditions, reactions, and trends influences every navigational decision you make. Be sure you know and understand navigation weather so you can evaluate and use the various methods of navigation accurately. The "metro" section usually provides good winds aloft and enroute weather, but you must realize that this is difficult because of the great distances involved and because of limited reporting facilities. "Hump" weather is a phenomenon by itself and China weather is often difficult to judge. There has been a great deal of instrument flying on missions in China and unpredicted wind shifts have caused trouble. Learn the weather of this area as well as you can because, as always, weather is the greatest factor affecting all sorts of navigation.

H. NAVIGATOR'S CHECK LIST

Before going on a mission, it is necessary for you to check carefully all your equipment and materials. The following navigator's check list is standard in this Command.

1. Pre–flight.

    a.   Mission data

        (1)   Complete flight plan with latest wind in log book or on special sheet provided by Group. Run over this with the crew.

           (a) ETA at target.

           (b) ETA at base.

           (c) Rendezvous

           (d) ETA in enemy territory in and out plus ETA at important enemy areas

           (e) Escape areas

        (2)   Charts prepared and checked.

        (3)   Celestial procedure for mission organized.

        (4)   Inspect and check communication and intelligence flimsies. Plot all radio aids, emergency landing fields, and important intelligence data on master chart.

    b.   Navigation Kit. Complete set of navigation equipment for celestial and dead-reckoning navigation anywhere in the intended operational area. This equipment will include:

        (1)   B6B computer

        (2)   Weems plotter

        (3)   Dividers, triangles, parallel rule (optional)

        (4)   A-13 chronometer

        (5)   A-11 hack watch

        (6)   A-3 stopwatch

        (7)   Current Air Almanac

        (8)   Necessary H.O. 218 or H.O. 214 chart

        (9)   Ageton or Dreisonstok and forms

        (10) Rude Star Finder

        (11) Supplementary blank forms, TMs, and H.O. publications.

    c.   Charts
- (1) Complete set of AAF Aeronautical Charts, International Map of the World Charts or similar charts, scale 1:1,000,000 for pilotage anywhere in the intended operational area.
- (2) All available AAF Aeronautical Charts, scale, 1:500,000 for pilotage anywhere in the general target area.
- (3) Necessary AAF Long Range Air Navigation Charts, scale, 1:3,000,000 or similar charts covering the entire operational area.
- (4) Sufficient 1:3,000,000 mercator plotting charts or V-P plotting charts.

    d.   Sextant and accessories
- (1) Check sextant for correction using either a stationary curve or a collimator
- (2) Check sextant batteries and light bulbs
- (3) Check bubble for operation
- (4) Check averaging device

    e.   Weather
- (1) Terminal forecasts
- (2) Route forecasts
- (3) Winds aloft

    f.   Correct time (time tick frequency)
- (1) Obtain time tick
- (2) List of frequencies from which to obtain time ticks
- (3) Chronometer rate

    g.   Astro compass aligned properly

    h.   All calibration cards. Date zeroed on deviation cards with dates of calibration displayed on master indicator and remote indicators for gyro-fluxgate compass.

2. Before take-off.
- a.   Check personal effects including clothing, parachute, life vest, flak suit, helmet, check CO_2 capsules, escape kit, and flashlight.

b. Synchronize all aircraft clocks and watches of crew members.
c. Check oxygen system.
d. Set altimeter 29.92 to read pressure altitude.
e. Gyro-fluxgate compass. Check to see
   (1) Uncages on "on" at all times
   (2) System is functioning
   (3) Compass sensitivity set properly
   (4) Spare fuses available
f. API functioning and set properly.

A USAAF reconnaissance photograph of Freising, Bavaria, taken following an attack on April 18, 1945. As this photograph suggests, features such as rivers and major highways were very useful points of orientation for bomber navigators. (USAAF)

3. During flight.
   a. Continually check and cross-check all navigation instruments.
       (1) Check T.H. with astro compass. Check CFC compass against the magnetic compass to see that CFC is operating correctly. See that CFC variation knob is at desired position.
       (2) Continually set proper data into CFC Gun Computer Handset.
       (3) See that IFF [identification friend or foe (system)] is on and off at the proper times.

   b. Enroute to target
       (1) Rendezvous control points must be made good in time, place, and altitude.
       (2) Inform crew when they may test-fire guns.
       (3) Constantly brief crew with respect to enemy territory and installations.

   c. Navigation in the target area.
       (1) Record as much as you can of energy aircraft, antiaircraft, observed damage, and formations.
       (2) Get a pinpoint before leaving the target area.

   d. Navigation to Home Base. This is the navigation that is by far the most difficult. You have to find your base in the middle of a large land mess without much help from terrain or radio aids. Just beyond your base are the biggest mountains in the world. You must never relax until you are on your field. You must constantly be prepared to make direct for an emergency field. Be sure you are squared away on the help you can get from your radio operator.

4. After landing.
   a. Check all switches and stow equipment.
   b. Give your reports to the proper authority.
   c. Interrogation
   d. Navigation analysis
   e. Turn in your charts and flimsies

[. . .]

VIII. RADIO PROCEDURE

A. INTRODUCTION

To be a good radio operator you must know the equipment you have to use while in flight, and what ground installations are available for you to contact. You are the crew member who is trained primarily as a radioman. In the event of an emergency, the lives of all your fellow crew members may depend on your ability. The other crew members will also expect you to answer their questions regarding the radio equipment carried in your airplane, and what goes on in the ground installations. The only way you can answer those questions is to know the equipment. Be eager. If you haven't seen the inside of a Direction Finding station or a control tower, go to visit one. Learn all about your equipment and its capabilities and practice using them. And then practice some more.

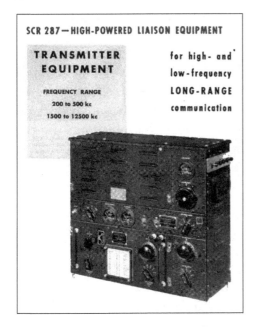

SCR 287—HIGH-POWERED LIAISON EQUIPMENT

TRANSMITTER EQUIPMENT

FREQUENCY RANGE
200 to 500 kc
1500 to 12500 kc

for high- and
low-frequency
LONG-RANGE
communication

B. AIRBORNE RADIO EQUIPMENT

1. Command Set.

The command set (SCR-274N) is primarily used for voice communication between the aircraft and control tower for airdrome control, and for command communication between aircraft when flying in formation. This is a multi-channel piece of equipment and normally three receivers and two transmitters are installed, with the third transmitter carried as a spare.

As a rule, one of the transmitters is tuned to the international control tower frequency (4495 kcs) and the other to the air-to-air command frequency assigned to your Group. Of the three receivers, one is used for monitoring control tower, beacon and range frequencies; the second is used to monitor the Group air-to-air command frequency; and the third remains unused or is tuned to the XX Bomber Command air-to-air command frequency. The transmitters each have an output of approximately 12 watts when used for voice transmission. However, they may also be used as Continuous Wave transmitters and have a keying circuit for this purpose. When used as a CW transmitter the peak power output is approximately 40 watts. This is a good point to remember if your liaison transmitter goes out, for by tuning one of the command set transmitters to the desired frequency, it may be used as a liaison transmitter for requesting D/F aid, clearances, etc.

2. Liaison Set.

The liaison set which consists of the AN/ART-13 radio transmitter and the BC-348( ) radio receiver is primarily used for contacting air-ground radio, stations other than the control tower. The receiver is a conventional superheterodyne receiver with a frequency range of 200 to 500 kilocycles and from 1.5 to 18.00 megacycles.

Radio transmitter AN/ART-13 is a ten channel pretuned transmitter with automatic tuning. The pilot is furnished with a remote control head and may select any of the ten channels at will. Frequencies to be setup are listed in SOI and generally include: The Group air-ground frequency, "route" frequencies to contact flight control stations and the international distress frequency of 500 kilocycles.

3. Radio Compass.

The Radio Compass SCR-269-G installed in B-29 aircraft is one of the most valuable aids to air-navigation carried in your airplane. It can be used to "home" on radio beacons or ranges or on any radio station which is broadcasting on a frequency which can be tuned in on the compass receiver. It can also be used to determine your position by taking a bearing on two or more radio stations whose identity and position can be established. The intersection of the bearings indicates the aircraft's position.

The radio compass employs two types of antennae, a loop antenna and a sense antenna. If the situation arises where the sense antenna becomes useless, a wire jumper between the antenna binding post of the radio compass and the antenna binding post of the antenna switching relay of the SCR-274N radio set, will enable the antenna of that set to be used as an emergency sense antenna.

All aircraft commanders are cautioned not to depend on enemy radio stations as a homing aid for use with the radio compass.

C. GROUND RADIO FACILITIES

1. Air-Ground Stations.

At both its Forward and Rear Area bases, each Group maintains an air-ground station for working the ships assigned to that Group. This is the normal ground contact for B-29 aircraft and should always be used for that purpose in preference to other installations. However, if the airplane commander deems it necessary, he may authorize you to contact any air-ground station available.

The XX Bomber Command maintains two air-ground radio stations which are operated by Army Airways Communications System. In India, this station is located at Kalaikunda transmitting and receiving on two CW [continuous wave—Morse signals] and two voice frequencies. It is used by transport aircraft in a manner similar to the B-29's use of the Group stations. The second Bomber Command station is located at Hsinching, China, and transmits and receives on two CW end four voice frequencies. This station, working with the Aircraft Traffic Control Center, controls all flights in the Hsinching area. B-29s are required to work this station while flying in China but are not required to work the station in India, though it may be contacted by B-29s if the need exists. The Air Transport Command maintains numerous air-ground stations throughout India. The stations of particular interest to aircraft of this Command are those along the "Hump" route. They stand by on normal "route" frequencies and furnish D/F aid and weather reports if requested.

In China the 14th Air Force maintains an elaborate fighter control net, with air-ground stations scattered all over Unoccupied China. In an emergency, these stations may be contacted on the common fighter control frequency. These stations can furnish local weather and may be of aid in locating position, or obtaining directions on course to fly, but they do not have D/F equipment.

Frequencies and call signs of XX Bomber Command installations are listed in XX Bomber Command SOI. Air Transport Command installations are listed in the ICD-ATC Radio Facility Chart which is carried in all Command aircraft. Fourteenth Air Force facilities are included in special briefing material. All information regarding air-ground facilities along the route flown will be given at preflight briefing.

2. Aids to Air-Navigation.

By far the most common aid to air-navigation is the radio beacon. This is nothing more than a low frequency transmitter emitting a continuous coded signal in a 360° field pattern, which may be homed on with the radio compass. All beacons in India-Burma and China Theatres use A-1 (CW) emission, so care must be taken to have the CW-Voice switch on the radio compass control box in the CW position when using a radio beacon. The frequencies, call signs, and locations of beacons are contained in the ICD-ATC Radio Facility Chart and in special briefing material.

The next most common aid to air-navigation is the radio range. These ranges are of the normal four quadrant coded type and are more common in India than in China. Frequencies, call signs, and locations of ranges are contained in the ICD-ATC Radio Facility Chart.

3. Direction Finding (D/F) Stations.

D/F stations are installed at all XX Bomber Command bases and at numerous ATC fields. The accuracy of the bearings they can "shoot" depends upon weather conditions as excessive atmospheric disturbances produce static effecting the accuracy of the D/F equipment. However, any inaccuracy caused by weather will be reflected in the class of bearing which is always given. There is a special procedure for contacting these stations and obtaining D/F aid which must be followed. [. . .]

4. Instrument Approach System.

There is installed at all bases of this Command a SCS-51 Instrument Approach System which may be used by B-29s in letting down under instrument conditions.

The system consists of a beamed transmitter which indicates the line of the runway, and of a series of fan marker beacons which indicate to an approaching aircraft the distance it is from the end of the runway. Carried in the aircraft is a marker beacon receiver which indicates when the fan marker beacons are passed over. Also carried is an indicator which by means of a swinging needle indicates whether the aircraft is to the right or left of the desired flight path along the runway. By using a predetermined rate of descent in conjunction with the beamed transmitter and marker beacons, a safe let-down can be made under conditions of low visibility.

As soon as additional equipment is available, a glide path transmitter will also be installed. An additional needle on the aircraft indicator will then show whether the aircraft is above or below the glide path which when followed will let the aircraft touch down at the end of the runway.

D. OPERATING PROCEDURES

1. Radio Telephone (R/T) Procedure.

Your voice messages must be kept short and to the point. Standard phraseology achieves this, and R/T speech should always be clear and slow, with an even emphasis on each word. Words must not be run together and messages will be spoken in natural phrases and not word by word. The phonetic alphabet will be used as an aid to more intelligible R/T procedure and will be used in spelling out words. The alphabet will be memorized and must be strictly adhered to.

    a.   Phonetic Alphabet
        A–Able
        B–Baker
        C–Charlie
        D–Dog
        E–Easy
        F–Fox
        G–George
        H–How
        I–Item

J-Jig
K-King
L-Love
M-Mike
N-Nan
O-Oboe
P-Peter
Q-Queen
R-Roger
S-Sugar
T-Tare
U-Uncle
V-Victor
W-William
X-Xray
Y-Yoke
Z-Zebra

b. Pronunciation of Numerals
   0 – Zero
   1 – Wun
   2 – Too
   3 – The-ree
   4 – Fo-wer
   5 – Fi-yiv
   6 – Six
   7 – Seven
   8 – Ate
   9 – Niner

c. Components of A Voice Message
   (1) The Call. For example, "Hello Uncle Sugar" (call sign of receiving station) this is Abraham" (call sign of calling: station).
   (2) Text (subject matter). Contains plain language, code words or figures. If it is necessary to spell a word use the phonetic alphabet.

(3) Ending. Every voice transmission must end with one of the following procedure words: (a) "OVER" meaning "My transmission is ended and I expect an answer from you." (b) "OUT" meaning "This conversation is ended and no reply is expected."

d. Transmitting and Answering

When both stations are in good communication all parts of the transmission are made once. When communication is difficult, phrases, words or groups may be repeated at the end of message or may be transmitted by using the procedure phrase "words twice". A group of figures will be transmitted in the ordinary manner using the "words twice" procedure if necessary.

Time of origin will be expressed in four digits and will be preceded by the word "TIME" (assuming that you are instructed to assign a time of origin to a voice message).

When words are missed or doubtful, repetitions will be requested by the receiving station before receipting for the message. The procedure phrases "Say again" or "I say again" will be used in conjunction with "all before," "all after", "word before" or "word after". EXAMPLE: "Hello Abraham, this is Charlie Uncle. Say again all after fifty. Over." "Hello Charlie Uncle, this is Abraham. I say again all after fifty. Seven three zero nine. Over."

When a word is required to be spelled to insure correct reception, the phrase "I spell" will be used immediately before beginning to spell the word in question.

A station is understood to have readability of good strength, unless otherwise notified. Except when making original contact, strength of signals and readability will not be exchanged unless one station cannot clearly hear another station. The response to "How do you hear me?" will be a short concise report of actual reception, such as "Weak but readable", "Strong but distorted", etc.

Procedure and priority designations are seldom used in voice transmissions. However, if it desired to use a priority designation, it will be spoken in the clear as the last part of the message.

In the interests of security, only those transmissions which are absolutely necessary will be made by R/T. No idle chatter will be engaged in. The more the enemy can hear the more he can find out about you.

e.   Procedure Phrases

Word or Phrase	Meaning
Roger	I have received all of your last transmission.
Acknowledge	Let me know that you have received and understand this message.
Wilco	Your last message received, understood and will be complied with.
How do you hear me?	How strong, and clear is my transmission?
Wait	If the pause required is longer than a few seconds, it must be followed by the ending "OUT."
Say again - I Say Again	When requesting the repetition of a previous transmission or used to preface a previous transmission. The word "REPEAT" is never used in this sense as it has a distinct operational meaning for the British Army.
Verify	Check coding, check text with the originator and send correct version.
Message for You	I wish to transmit a message to you.
Send Your Message	Go ahead, transmit.
Read Back	Repeat this message back to me exactly as received after I give "OVER."
That is Correct	You are correct.
Words Twice	(1) As a request: Communication is difficult, send every phrase (or code group) twice. (2) As information: Since communication is difficult, I will send every phrase (or code group) twice.
Correction	An error has been made in this transmission (or message indicated). The correct version is _____.

Wrong	What you have just heard is the incorrect version. The correct version is _____.
Groups	The number of groups in this code or cipher message is _____.
Break	I hereby indicate the separation of the text from other portions of the message. This word is used only when there is not a clear distinction between the text and other portion of a message.

Crew Survival

The Air Force *magazine account of the final action of B-17 Old 666, operating with the 65th Bombardment Squadron, 43rd Bombardment Group, in the Pacific, gives a strong sense of the drama involved in one particular mission, although doubtless with a nod to morale it omits to clarify that one of the aircrew died in addition to five being wounded. Furthermore, crew reports of downing five Japanese aircraft were overstatements—one Zero ditched due to engine failure and three others were damaged by the B-17's gunfire. Dramatic overstatement of kills was common, although given the high emotion of combat operations this tendency was often down to adrenaline distortions of memory rather than outright falsification. Note how in this account every crew member is a true combatant.*

Old 666 took off from a South Pacific airdrome one morning like any able-bodied B-17 and came back a pile of salvage wallowing through the sky. There wasn't much of her that hadn't been shot up and her bandaged crew resembled a rehearsal in first aid.

It was a reconnaissance flight over Bougainville Island and while photographing the Buka runway the crew spotted a string of enemy lighters, about twenty. Half of them taxied out on the strip to take off. But Old 666 headed south along the west side of the island and kept right on taking pictures.

The first fighter moved in, then three more, one sailing in low at ten o'clock. Fire from his guns wounded the bombardier, the pilot and the engineer, destroyed the hydraulic system, damaged the control cables smashed the pilot's rudders, set the oxygen bottles in the cockpit alight and knocked out all flight instruments but the airspeed indicator.

The bombardier, despite his wounds, kept firing on the enemy fighter until it shattered apart. The navigator, though wounded in the face and unable to see his target, blasted away at another attacker while the pilot, wounded in the legs and arms, continued to fire a fixed gun at still another Zero.

An explosive shell crashed through the nose of Old 666 and knocked the bombardier and navigator back into the catwalk under the cockpit. A burst of small caliber slugs from the same enemy plane wounded the radio operator and sewed a seam of holes in the fin. The engineer, wounded in both legs, kept his guns firing short bursts as he cleared them of repeated jams,

Despite his wounds and loss of blood, the pilot remained at the controls and managed to dodge some of the enemy and to maneuver the plane so his gunners could get cracks at the others for more than forty minutes. In this time at least five of the enemy were destroyed.

Once Old 666 had dived to low altitude, the navigator ripped out the oxygen bottles and extinguished the flames. When the attack finally ended the co-pilot set the throttles and turned the controls over to flight engineer who had told none of the crew of his own wounds. With only airspeed indicator and magnetic compass to guide him, the engineer flew Old 666 for an hour and a half while the co-pilot and the few uninjured members of the crew administered first aid to the others.

The radio operator, severely wounded in the neck, continued to secure bearings and brought the big plane home. On reaching the airdrome the co-pilot took over the controls and found it impossible to lower the flaps. He nevertheless brought her in.

It was her final landing—she was grounded after that—but Old 666 got down and rolled in gently to spare her wounded further pain.

CHAPTER 5

Gunners

In total, between 1941 and 1945 297,000 men graduated from the USAAF's gunnery schools. For many of these men, gunnery was not their only job—depending on the aircraft, the gunner might also be serving as a bombardier, navigator, radioman, or flight engineer (note that all enlisted men aboard a bomber would be trained aerial gunners). But whatever else they did on board, when enemy fighters attacked, these men were expected to climb into their turrets or take grip of their flexibly mounted machine gun, and attempt to fight off the nimble, lethal opponents.

The volume of defensive firepower aboard a bomber depended heavily on the type of aircraft. If we look at a light bomber such as the A-26B Invader, much of its firepower was offensively arranged in the nose or in optional wing pods; defensive armament consisted of two .50-cal M2 machine guns in a remote-control dorsal turret and the same in a remote-control ventral turret. At the other end of the scale, the B-17 Flying Fortress positively bristled with .50-cal guns. The B-17G had 13 such guns in total: twin guns in a chin turret; two individual guns on the nose cheeks; two on the waist of the fuselage; twin guns each in the upper turret, belly ball turret, and tail turret; and one firing upwards from the radio compartment behind the bomb bay. In August 1942, the USAAF toyed with the idea of developing an even more heavily gunned B-17 as a "destroyer escort," without a bombload and designed purely as a long-range escort gunship for the bomber formations. The idea bore practical fruit in the YB-40 aircraft, which flew a small number of sorties in 1943, but it was not a tactically sound proposition, not least because Luftwaffe fighters tended to zone in one straggling aircraft separated from the pack, and thus not protected by the destroyers. With the introduction of round-mission long-range fighter escorts in 1944, such a concept was void.

Gunner's Information File—Flexible Gunnery illustrates one point very clearly—aerial gunnery was technically and logically very difficult. The geometrical and physical principles of hitting an external moving object (the enemy fighter) from a moving platform (the bomber) with a stream of flying and arcing projectiles were not simple to acquire in either theory or practice. New gunners had to train themselves out of the perfectly natural instinct to aim their sights dead center on the enemy aircraft; such would simply result in their shots flying well past the tails of most fighters. The gunners also had to cope with the fact that they themselves were targets; enemy fighters would particularly target tail, upper, and belly turrets, as destroying these and killing the gunner inside would produce a bomber blind spot to exploit in further attacks. Nevertheless, the combined firepower of multiple heavy bombers did pose a significant threat to Axis fighters. Eighth Air Force bombers, for example, claimed 6,259 enemy aircraft destroyed, 1,836 probables, and 3,210 damaged. Although the actual figures might be notably less than these (adrenaline-fueled air gunners were liable to exaggeration), the cost to enemy aircraft was still appreciable.

From *Gunner's Information File—Flexible Gunnery* (1944)

YOUR GUN AND YOUR JOB

The standard United States aerial gun—your gun—is the air-cooled caliber .50 Browning machine gun.

Your job is to become enough of a machine gun expert to use and care for the gun properly and to make emergency repairs—so that no attacking fighter will ever catch you unable to fight back. This book and your instructors will show you how to do the job.

The first dozen pages are a general introduction to the gun. They define some of the words used in describing it. They identify the major groups of parts and tell how to take them out of the gun. They show briefly how the gun works and how to load, fire, and unload it safely.

The rest of the machine gun section discusses in detail every important part of the gun and the function it performs. It explains in pictures how

Just discernible in the center of this photo are two German fighters angling into attack on a formation of B-17F bombers during U.S. attacks on AGO Flugzeugwerke at Oschersleben, Germany, on July 28, 1943. (NARA)

to take the gun completely apart, how to adjust it, clean it, and oil it, and how to mount it on the adapter that holds it while it is firing.

As a final preparation for combat, the book tells how to load the ammunition, how to check the gun regularly for wear or damage, and how to locate the cause of trouble if the gun stops firing.

Brief descriptions of the caliber .30 machine gun and the caliber .45 automatic pistol, which aerial gunners also use at times, are added.

GUN TALK … terms and definitions you should know.

Your gun fires 750 to 850 shots a minute—14 shots a second. The bullets, weighing nearly two ounces each, leave the barrel at 1,977 miles an hour-2,900 feet a second. This speed is called the **muzzle velocity**. Even at a distance of four miles—the gun's **maximum range**—one of those bullets will kill a man.

At closer distances, the bullets wreck anything that gets in the way. In tests on the proving ground, the caliber .50 smashes through the metal skin and framework of an airplane, drills through a metal ammunition box, penetrates a hard pine board—and still has enough power left to pierce a plate of armor nearly a half inch thick.

Yet the gun is light—only 64 pounds—and small enough to fit into almost any airplane. The gun is an **automatic** weapon. After the first cartridge is loaded and the gun is cocked—an operation called **charging**—it will keep firing as long as the trigger is held down. A **semi-automatic** weapon, like the caliber .45 pistol, fires only one shot each time the trigger is squeezed.

Your caliber .50 is a **free**, or **flexible** gun—mounted so that it can be swung from side to side or up and down to fire in any direction. A **fixed** gun, like the machine guns in the wings of a fighter plane, cannot be moved—the whole plane must be turned to aim the gun.

The aircraft caliber .50 gun is **air-cooled**—air, circulating through the holes in the barrel jacket, keeps the barrel from heating up too fast. This system is effective because the air at high altitudes is very cold and the gun is sticking out into the slipstream. On the ground, the air-cooled gun heats up more rapidly and long bursts cannot be fired without damaging the barrel. Machine guns designed for ground use are water-cooled, or have a heavy barrel that can stand more heat.

Along the inside of the barrel—called the bore—are twisting **grooves**. The wide ridges between the grooves are called **lands**, and the grooves and lands together are called the **rifling**. It makes the bullet spin like a football in a good forward pass. Without it, the bullet would travel like a wobbly pass and the gun would lose most of its accuracy. The **caliber** of any gun is the distance across the inside of the barrel, measured from land to land. Your gun is a caliber .50 because the barrel is 50/100ths of an inch wide—in other words, half an inch. The bullet is a hair's breadth wider than half an inch. This makes for a tight fit which prevents any force from escaping when the shot is fired, and also squeezes the bullet into the grooves.

The **cartridge**, or **round** [. . .] While it is being fired, it is held in an enlarged opening called the **chamber** at the rear of the barrel.

The **cartridge case** is simply a metal shell. Near its base it has an **extracting groove** so that parts inside the gun can pull it out of the ammunition belt and then pull it out of the chamber after it has been fired.

Inside the case are the **primer** and the **propelling charge**. The primer is a small charge of high explosive which goes off when the gun's firing pin strikes it. This sets fire to the propelling charge, which burns-out in a flash and sends the bullet, or projectile, on its way.

The gases created by the propelling charge set up the terrific **chamber pressure** of 50,000 pounds, or 25 tons, per square inch inside the cartridge case—as much force as a medium tank balanced on a man's thumb.

Some of this force is absorbed by the barrel. Five tons drive the bullet forward. Another five tons give a backward kick—the **recoil**—to the empty case and some of the gun parts. After the **recoiling parts** are driven back as far as they can go, they bounce against springs and buffers that start them forward again. The forward movement is the **counter recoil**. As soon as the moving parts have returned to place, the gun is back in **battery position** and ready to fire again. To feed into the gun, the cartridges or rounds are hooked together with **metal links** to form a long ammunition belt. By changing certain parts of the gun, you can feed the belt from either side. After each shot, the empty cartridge case is pushed out the bottom of the gun, while the used links are tossed out to one side.

[. . .]

HANDLING YOUR GUN

Operating the gun, when it is properly set up and in good working order, is almost as easy as using a rifle. The methods shown here are simple, correct-and safe. They are designed to prevent accidents. Make a habit of doing the steps in this order.

CHARGING

Charging the gun-by pulling back the charging handle-cocks the firing pin. When there is an ammunition belt in place, it also moves around from the feedway into the chamber and moves the next round in the belt into place against the cartridge stops. Before the gun is loaded, charge it once without any ammunition in it and press the trigger to make sure the firing mechanism works. You should hear a click as the firing pin snaps forward. There is no use loading a gun that won't fire.

The correct way to charge the gun is also the easiest way:

1. Hold the grip **with your palm up**.
2. With one smooth and rapid movement, pull back and down on the grip, draw it all the way back, and let go. Pull **hard and fast**. A strong, steady pull may not break the gun out of battery. A strong, quick pull will.
3. Don't stop pulling when the grip is all the way back. Your arm should come back with such force that it keeps traveling back after the grip is forced out of your palm. This bounces the bolt against the back plate and helps the driving spring force it fully forward into battery position. **Above all, don't hold on to the grip and ride it forward**.

LOADING

Every gun you fire will be mounted in an adapter. After charging the gun to test the firing mechanism, put the safety on the adapter in the SAFE position while loading the gun.

Always feed the ammunition belt into the gun **with a double link entering first**.

To load a hand-held gun, or a turret gun whose cover can be raised:

1. Raise the cover and lift up the extractor assembly.
2. Put the first round firmly against the cartridge stops, with the double loop of the link projecting beyond the stops.
3. Put the extractor assembly down, see that its hook is in the extracting groove of the round, and close the cover, making sure it is latched.
4. Charge the gun once. This will move the first round from the feedway into the chamber.

To load a gun when you cannot raise the cover:

1. Push the end of the belt into the feedway until the first round is held in place by the belt holding pawl—the little catch on the bottom of the feedway.
2. Charge the gun twice. The first charging will move the round over against the cartridge stops; the second charging will move it into the chamber.

FIRING

To fire, squeeze the trigger and hold it back as long as you want the gun to keep firing. If the adapter has two triggers, you can fire by squeezing either of them or both.

The correct position of your head, arms, and body will be demonstrated on the firing range.

UNLOADING

To unload the gun before the ammunition belt is used up:

1. Raise the cover, lift the extractor assembly, and pull out the ammunition belt. If you have trouble removing the ammunition belt, shake it.
2. Charge the gun once to eject the live round left in the chamber.
3. Pull the bolt back and look into the T-slot and chamber to make sure they are empty. To make doubly sure, charge the gun once more.
4. Pull the trigger to release the firing pin. Put the safety on the adapter in the *SAFE* position.

When you continue firing until all the ammunition is used:

1. Pull back the bolt and make sure the T-slot and chamber are empty. Charge the gun once to be doubly sure.
2. Pull the trigger to release the firing pin. Put the safety on the adapter in the *SAFE* position.

SAFETY RULES

Never forget that a caliber .50 machine gun is essentially a terrific explosion wrapped up in a metal package.

When the gun is handled properly, it controls that explosion so that nobody can be hurt but the enemy.

But one instant of carelessness may release that packaged power at the wrong time, or in the wrong direction.

Never let that happen to you. Make these safety rules your safety bible.

Before Loading the Gun

Make sure the barrel is free of obstructions and excess oil.

Make sure the cover and back plate are securely latched.

Test the operation of the gun with dummy ammunition, or by hand charging and "dry firing" without any ammunition in the gun.

Put the safety on the adapter in the SAFE position.

While Firing the Gun

If, while you are pulling the trigger, the gun stops firing before the ammunition is used up, beware of a delayed explosion. Wait 10 seconds before charging the gun or raising the cover.

Never use a metal tool to pry a live round or an empty case out of the gun.

After Unloading

Make sure the chamber and T-slot are empty by charging the gun twice.

Release the firing pin and put the safety on the adapter in the *SAFE* position.

In the Shop

Check the chamber and T-slot before starting to work on the gun.

Never charge the gun against the pressure of the driving spring when the back plate is off.

Keep your fingers out of the gun when charging it with the cover raised.

Never try to force the parts when stripping or assembling the gun.

Make sure the cocking lever is forward before replacing the bolt in the receiver.

Make sure the bolt is in battery position before closing the cover.

Never lay a gun down where it may fall.

[. . .]

THE GUN IS ITS OWN TOOL KIT

In an emergency, the gun can be stripped with nothing but its own parts as tools.

Use the point of a cartridge or the cocking lever pin to depress the oil buffer body spring lock.

Use the cocking lever pin to drift out the sear stop pin and accelerator pin.

Use the flat tip of the cocking lever as you would use a screwdriver to remove and replace the sear stop, oil buffer tube lock, the cover latch spring, and cover extractor spring.

Use the oil buffer tube lock to pry the handle of the trigger bar pin out of its hole in the side of the receiver.

Use the sear stop pin to drift out the belt feed pawl pin.

But use these methods only when absolutely necessary and take care not to damage the parts used as tools. Never use the driving spring rod assembly as a tool.

HEATERS

In bombing missions at high altitude, where the temperature may drop to 50 degrees below zero, an electric heater is sometimes clamped over the cover of the gun to keep the parts from "freezing" together.

There are two models of the heater—one with a side plate extending down the left side of the gun, the other with the side plate on the right. The part that extends down must be opposite the charging handle.

To install a heater, turn its two clamps straight up. Raise the cover of the gun and slide the heater down on it as far as it will go. Turn the top clamp down and back until it snaps into the catch; turn the lower clamp up and back into the catch.

The heater turns on when you plug it into the bomber's electric output. Do not leave the heater connected when it is off the gun.

[. . .]

SIGHTING AND SIGHTS

DON'T SHOOT FROM THE HIP . . .

In the excitement of combat too many gunners spray their bullets at the enemy like a movie cowboy shooting from the hip. **Don't do it**. Use your sight—and use it correctly—or you won't stand a chance of hitting. You will only throw away ammunition on which your life may depend. Firing a gun from a fast moving bomber is far different from shooting on the ground. Except for one very rare case, you can't possibly hit a fighter by pointing your gun straight at him. You must aim a certain distance away, called **deflection**. To apply the right amount of deflection you use your sight. Two main types of sights are used by air gunners. **Computing sights** calculate the deflection automatically. You make certain adjustments. The sight does the rest. [. . .]

But if you have **ring sights**, you must measure off the deflection yourself. You can only do so by using the accurate and combat tested method of aiming called **Position Firing** [. . .] Ring sights fall into two classes. One kind—the iron sight—is simply an iron ring near the back of the gun which you line up with a bead on a post at the front of the gun. The other kind—the optical sight—uses a system of lenses to make the ring, the center bead and the enemy fighter all appear on the same glass screen.

Some sights, both iron and optical, have one ring. Others have two rings, and the newest have three rings. But Position Firing works with all of them, regardless of the number of rings. This section is illustrated with a three ring optical. One you know all the rules of Position Firing, you will have no trouble applying them with any other type of sign sight. The principle remains the same. Always remember that no matter how good a shot you are on the ground, you can never shoot down an enemy fighter who is making a continuous attack on you unless you **use your**

sights correctly and follow the rules of Position Firing. There is one exception—dumb luck—and that isn't good enough. The enemy may be lucky first.

POSITION FIRING

When the fighter attacks . . .

When you see an enemy fighter [. . .] with his guns blazing, you won't have time to think about the rules of Position Firing. You will have to know them so well that you act as quickly and automatically as your gun.

Fortunately, Position Firing boils down to three simple rules. They have been proved in combat and scientifically checked. They work—better than any other system of sighting.

You may run into gunners who use other methods or no method at all. However, if there is a ring sight on your gun, this is the way to use it against a fighter making a direct and continuous attack on you.

If you follow the rules of Position Firing, you can get your mission through and get yourself safely home. But you will have to know these rules letter-perfect, and practice them until they become second nature.

. . . he is a flying gun

To understand Position Firing, it is necessary to know what the fighter does when he attacks a bomber.

His guns are fixed. They are mounted in his wings and fuselage, pointing straight ahead. To aim them, he must aim his entire plane. He is really nothing but a flying gun. To hit you, he must point his nose at a spot ahead of the nose of your bomber, so that his bullets will be there by the time you get there.

To do this he can make a **fly-through attack**, or he can fly a **pursuit curve**.

Fly-through attacks . . .

are as simple as this picture indicates. The fighter flies in a straight line and fires at a point he expects your bomber to cross. He lays down a screen of fire and hopes that you will fly through it.

Sometimes he comes in from the side, like this. Often he comes in from the front and slams right through the bomber formation. Usually his chief object is to break up the formation or to cripple one bomber so that he can pick it off when it straggles. But his aim is correct for only an instant.

Pursuit curve attacks . . .

. . . develop like this. They are the standard type of fighter attack, and the most dangerous.

Instead of intercepting your bomber with his bullets for just a single instant, the fighter tries to keep pouring a constant stream of bullets at you.

To do this he must continue to point just ahead of the bomber's nose. He must keep turning in the direction the bomber is flying. His path

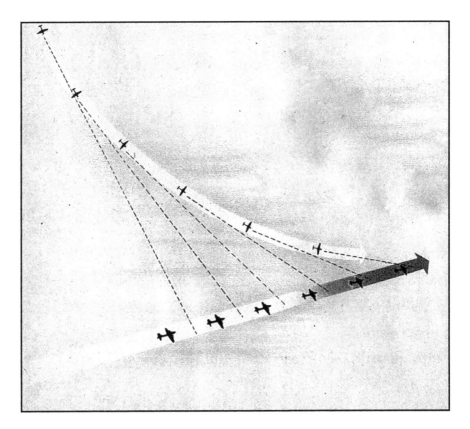

becomes a smooth curve. He has no choice—either he flies the curve or his bullets won't keep hitting.

Because you know that he must fly this curve, he becomes an easy shot. Position Firing tells you how to hit him on that curve.

A typical pursuit curve: the fighter does this

As the fighter follows a pursuit curve, continually pointing his guns just ahead of the bomber, he moves closer and closer until he slides in behind the bomber's tail. Since the fighter is faster, he quickly closes in. Finally he gets so close that he must break off the attack.

This is the real motion of a fighter on a pursuit curve from the beam, straight out from the side of the bomber, as it would be seen from another plane high overhead.

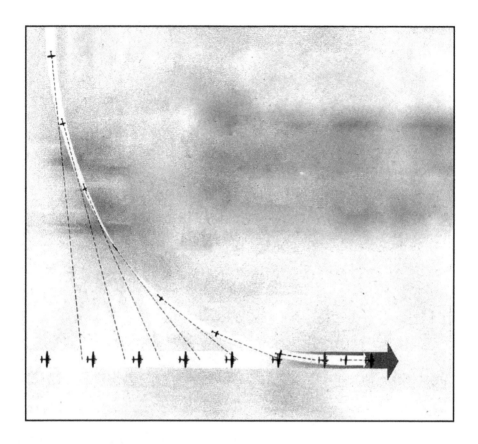

A typical pursuit curve: the gunner sees this

To the gunner, the fighter flying a pursuit curve always appears just about head-on. This is the one sure way to spot an attack.

Although the fighter really flies in a curve, he always looks to you as though **he slides sideways, in a straight line, toward your bomber's tail**. This is the line of the fighter's **apparent motion**.

He also keeps getting bigger, because he is coming closer—fast. To you in the bomber, the beam attack above looks like this.

Fighters will try anything . . .

They may come in from the side, the nose, or the tail, or even from overhead. But all these attacks have one thing in common. No matter from what direction the fighter approaches, he must maneuver into a position where he can get his guns bearing on you.

To keep them bearing he must fly a pursuit curve.

That is the part of the attack where he is really dangerous to you, and fortunately, that's where Position Firing makes him easiest for you to hit.

Remember, you are moving too . . .

This is not as self-evident as it seems, because when you are flying in a bomber, you're rarely conscious of your own motion.

But the simple fact that you are moving at high speed is of the greatest importance in learning where to aim.

Believe it or not—

Your bullets do not go where you point your gun.

The newsboy's lesson...

Every newsboy soon learns the basic trick of aiming from his moving bicycle. The first time he tosses a newspaper he discovers a simple fact: if he aims directly at a front porch, he misses, and the paper lands next door. The forward motion of his bicycle carries the newspaper forward, too.

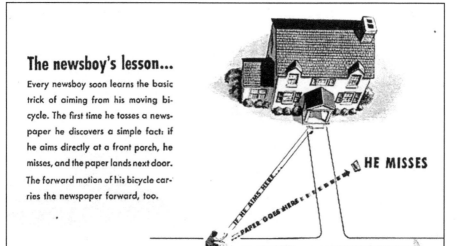

To hit the porch, the newsboy must aim like this

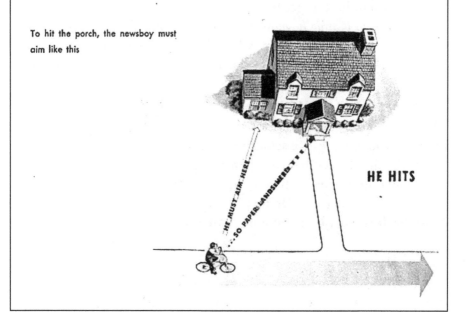

...applies to bombers, too

The same thing happens to a bullet fired from a moving plane. Before the bullet is fired, it is carried forward in the same direction as the bomber.

When the gun is fired, the bullet shoots out of the barrel in a different direction. As soon as it leaves the muzzle, the bullet turns and follows a path between those two directions. It keeps the forward motion given it by the moving bomber.

You will miss if you fly over a field and shoot like this at a fighter on the ground.

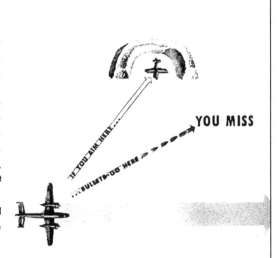

YOU MISS

To hit, you must aim like this.

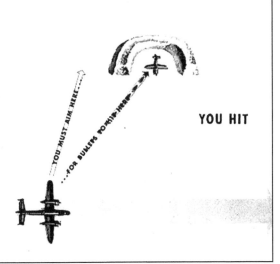

YOU HIT

Hitting a moving fighter...

If the fighter is moving toward your bomber, you must still allow for the forward motion of your bullet.

If you aim at a point ahead of the moving fighter, as you aim ahead of a running fox, you will miss. Your bullets, carried forward, will pass in front of the fighter.

YOU MISS

To hit, you must aim like this. Then the fighter and your bullets will arrive at the same place at the same time.

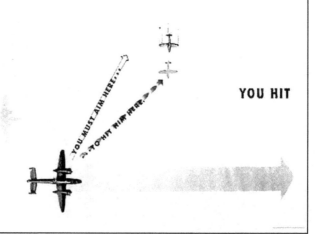

YOU HIT

Hitting a fighter on a pursuit curve...

If the bomber and fighter are both in the air, and the fighter is making a pursuit curve attack, the same principle holds.

If you try to lead ahead of a fighter, as you ordinarily would aim at a flying duck, you will miss, because your bullet, carried forward by your own speed, goes ahead of him.

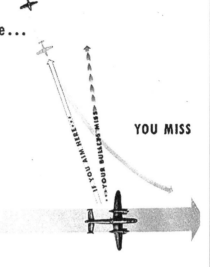

YOU MISS

To hit you must aim like this. Position Firing corrects for the distance your bullet is carried forward so that it will meet the fighter instead of passing in front of him.

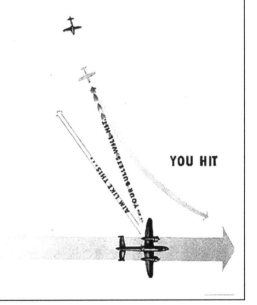

YOU HIT

Where you aim . . .

You have seen in the preceding pages, that if you shoot in any direction other than dead ahead or dead astern, your bullets do **not** go where you aim. The bullets not only move away from your gun, but they are also carried forward and they are carried forward regardless of whether you fire to the side, above, or below.

Like the boy on the bicycle, you must always allow for this forward motion. Make this allowance by using the **first rule** of Position Firing:

> **Always aim between the attacking fighter and the tail of your own bomber along the line of the fighter's apparent motion**

This line of his apparent motion is always in the general direction of that spot on the horizon toward which your bomber's tail points.

Rads . . .

The amount you must aim away from the fighter is called **deflection**. It is measured in **Rads**—the distance between the center and the inner ring, or the distance between two rings in your 35 mil rad sight.

The right deflection

varies from 3 to 0 rads and depends on the direction of the fighter's attack.

Therefore the **second rule** is:

> **Use the right amount of deflection**

When you fire at a 90 degree angle—straight out from the beam—you must make the maximum allowance of 3 rads for the amount the bullet is carried forward.

When you fire straight ahead or straight behind, the forward motion of your bomber does not change the direction of your bullet; therefore, the deflection is 0, or point blank.

At any other angle in between, the right amount of deflection is somewhere between 3 and 0 rads.

Learn the deflections for the key directions of attack shown alongside.

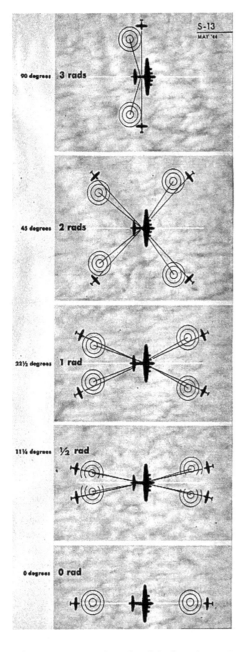

The number of Rads . . .

always depends on the fighter's angle to your fore and aft axis.

It makes no difference whether the fighter attacks from the right side or the left . . . or whether he attacks from above or below.

When the fighter attacks from a certain angle he may be at your level, or he may be above you or below you. But it's still the same angle. Think of that angle as rotating around the fore and aft axis of your bomber so that it forms the surface of a cone.

The cones tell you the deflection . . .

Think of the key directions of attack as surfaces of cones which go out into the sky around your bomber, both behind and in front of you.

Remember these imaginary cones by their numbers—½, 1, 2, 3. The number of the cone gives you the deflection in rads for any fighter on the surface of that cone, whether he attacks from the right or the left; high, level, or low.

To hit any attacking fighter on cone ½—just off your fore-and-aft axis—use ½ rad of deflection. For any fighter on cone 1, use 1 rad, and for any fighter on cone 2, use 2 rads of deflection. The 3-rad

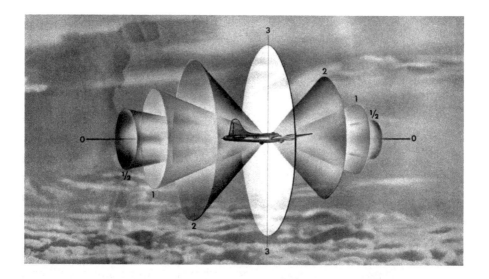

position-at right angles to your line of flight—is a wheel rather than a cone. But the same rule applies: for any fighter in this position, use 3 rads of deflection.

Know your true airspeed . . .

Changes in the speed of the fighter on the pursuit curve do not change your deflection. **But changes in your true airspeed do change your deflection.**

The deflections shown above are correct for a 225 m.p.h. true airspeed of the bomber.

For each 50 m.p.h. increase in bomber's speed, increase deflection ½ rad.

For each 50 m.p.h. decrease in bomber's speed, decrease deflection ½ rad.

Check your true airspeed with the navigator or bombardier.

The illustrations on these two pages demonstrate how to apply Rules 1 and 2—using the three-ring optical sight which is shown in all the drawings in this section. Note, on both pages, how the deflection is laid off in the direction of the tail of your bomber (Rule 1).

Note also how all fighters coming from the same angle are given the same deflection (Rule 2) —regardless of whether they come from above, below, or to one side. All the fighters on these two pages are on cone 1 and take a 1 rad deflection.

The tail gunner aims like this . . .

On tail attacks you always aim inside the fighter. When he dives on you, aim below him. When he climbs on you, aim above him. In these illustrations, of course, the sliding motion of the fighter toward the bomber's tail cannot be seen. But the point of aim has been placed along his line of apparent motion.

In attacks from the front, the fighter's line of apparent motion is still in the direction of your bomber's tail. If you have trouble thinking of

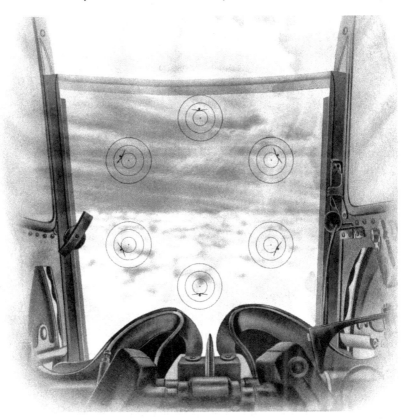

aiming in the direction of the tail, just remember to aim away from your bomber's nose-which is the same thing.

The nose gunner aims like this . . .

On frontal attacks, you always aim **outside** the fighter. When he dives on you, aim above him. When he climbs on you, aim below him.

Deflection changes during an attack . . .

The fighter never stays on one cone. His pursuit curve always forces him closer to the bomber's tail. During the attack, he moves from one cone to another—and he moves fast. In a **beam attack**, where the fighter starts at the 3-rad position, he drifts to the 2-rad position, then to the 1-rad position and finally to the ½-rad position.

Unless you change your deflection as the fighter's angle changes, your aim becomes wrong almost immediately.

So the **third rule** of Position Firing is:

Change your deflection during the attack

This is not easy to do. Get all the practice you can. Remember that the trick is to swing your guns smoothly, like a good batter swinging at a pitched ball.

On all attacks from side or rear, let the fighter drift to the center of your sight.

He is on your beam at right angles. Give him 3 rads.
As he slides to Cone 2, reduce your deflection to 2 rads.
He swings to Cone 1. Follow through smoothly to give him 1 rad.
As he moves to Cone ½, let him slip in to ½ rad.

[. . .]

If a fighter starts a **nose attack** on Cone ½, he will move very quickly to Cone 1 and even faster toward Cone 2—if he can hold his pursuit curve that long without blacking out.

On attacks from the front, let the fighter drift away from the center of your sight

When he's on Cone ½, you give him ½ rad.
He changes to Cone 1. Let him drift out to the 1 rad ring.
As he whips toward Cone 2, increase deflection to 2 rads.

You've got to be on the ball—or else.

No bomber is safe unless each gunner searches the sky constantly throughout each mission. Search systematically and continuously the portion of sky assigned to you, especially in the sun and in broken clouds, where fighters like to hide. Be ready for any trick from any fighter you see. You are responsible for seeing that your airplane is never surprised.

Bombers and their crews have been needlessly lost because gunners were not watching and let fighters sneak in on them.

The clock system . . .

. . . has nothing to do with the cones. You use it to tell the entire crew when there are enemy fighters in the sky, and exactly where they are.

Simply think of your bomber as flying in the center of a huge clock, with the nose pointed toward 12 o'clock and the tail toward 6 o'clock.

If you imagine the hand of this imaginary clock pointing at a fighter you want to locate, the hand will show at what "o'clock" that fighter is.

If you are a tail gunner, don't be confused by the fact that you are riding backward. You are facing 6 o'clock. 3 o'clock is on your left, 9 o'clock is on your right.

When you spot an enemy, sound off . . .

1. How many fighters and the type. For Germans the number is usually enough. "two one-o-nines".
2. At what "o'clock" the fighter is.
3. "High", "level", or "low", depending on whether the fighter is above your bomber, at the same level, or below.
4. "Coming in"—but only when he really turns into the attack.

For the top fighter in the picture call:
    One 109.—10:30 o'clock.—High.
For the right hand fighter call:
    One 109.—3 o'clock.—Level.—Coming in!
For the bottom fighter call:
    One 190.—7 o'clock.—Low

Never fail to sound off when fighters appear, because you may be the only one who sees them.

No single crew member can see all the sky around the bomber from his turret or window. Even the pilot can see very little except straight ahead. Your warning may be the crew's only notice of an attack. It will help other gunners bring their guns to bear and will allow the pilot to take the necessary evasive action.

On the other hand, don't jam the interphone with excited double talk. Be sure to say "coming in", but **only** when the fighter really turns in. Otherwise you may have the whole crew swinging their guns at a plane a mile away, while some smart fighter slips in and picks you off.

Some pilots may want you to call "in range" when the fighter is about to get his guns bearing, to guide them in any special evasive action they may wish to take.

When to fire . . .

Expert studies show that aerial machine guns are most effective at ranges up to 600 yards. Very careful calculations prove that further out bullets scatter so widely that they make your chances of a hit almost entirely a matter of luck. You can't hope to break even on the game that way.

Most fighters who are any good won't open up on you outside of 600 yards. A good fighter pilot may wait until he is much closer. Watch him through your ring sight. Be ready with the right deflection and let him have it at 600 yards. Nose attacks are so fast that you should begin shooting when he's lined up on you normally at 900–1000 yards.

The exact time to start firing and the proper length of burst to fire depend on combat conditions. They are determined, in each theater, by the type of mission usually flown, ammunition loads, and enemy tactics.

The 8th Air Force, for example, instructs gunners to start shooting as soon as the fighter is head on, short bursts at first, longer ones as he gets within 600 yards. These methods work over Germany. Bursts at longer range than 600 yards have been known to scare fighters away. On long missions the length of bursts must be kept short to conserve ammunition. You can't afford to be left with empty ammunition cans.

If you do run out of ammunition, or your guns fail, keep swinging them at the enemy anyway. Never let them know that you can't hurt them—or they'll be all over you.

You can tell the range . . .

By the size of the fighter in the 35 mil rad of your sight. At 600 yards the average single-engine fighter fills about ½ rad in your ring sight. Most twin-engine fighters fill ⅞ of a rad. The JU 88 fills a full rad.

Range	Average single-engine fighters	Average twin-engine fighters	JU 88 twin-engine fighter
600 yards	½ rad	⅞ rad	1 rad
1,000 yards	⅓ rad	½ rad	⅝ rad

When you spot a fighter, or get warning over the interphone, be ready for anything

There's no use kidding yourself. Enemy fighter pilots are good. They know every trick in the book.

The enemy has good planes, and pilots who know how to get everything out of them. Fighter pilots will take advantage of all their strong points—such as armor plating, speed, maneuverability. They will look for any weak points on your bomber or your formation—such as a gun position which is not firing, or a spot with the fewest guns bearing on them. When a bomber is crippled or straggles out of position, they will attack it viciously.

A smart fighter pilot will also use weather. He will sneak out of a cloud or out of the sun-trying to get in close before you can see him.

Often fighters will gang up. One fighter, or several, will make fake attacks to draw your attention. In the meantime, the real attack will come from somewhere else.

Against these tactics, your best defense is to keep alert—and to keep calm at the same time. Watch every enemy fighter carefully, but don't let him trick you in to firing at him when you don't have a chance.

[. . .]

OVERTAKING

The fighter flies a parallel course with the bomber, usually more than 1000 yards away. He continues this until he reaches the right point for his . . .

TURN IN

The fighter banks sharply for a turn that will bring his guns to bear slightly ahead of your nose. For a moment he seems to hang motionless in the air-his far wing up, as though hanging from a hook.

ROLL THROUGH

He has now turned toward you but must still reverse his turn to get his guns bearing. As he does this, he rolls his high wing down, which brings him to the beginning of . . .

GUNS BEARING

This is where you get him. Rapidly growing larger as he comes closer, he appears to slide back toward your tail.

BREAKAWAY

When he decides to break off, the fighter sometimes makes a climbing, but more often a diving turn. He frequently rolls over on his back to expose his armored belly as he tries to get away and into position for a new attack.

SIDE attack . . .

The side attack is usually used against single bombers, rarely against formations. It can be made from above, at, or slightly below your level.

This drawing shows a high side attack from the beam, with the fighter getting his guns bearing about 600 yards out. To press the attack home to close range, he must drift well into your tail cone where you have an even better crack at him than he has at you.

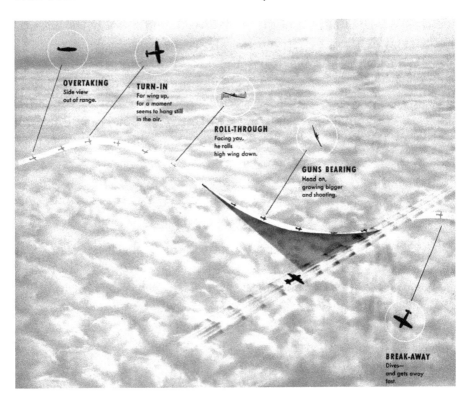

OVERTAKING
Side view
out of range.

TURN-IN
Far wing up,
for a moment
seems to hang still
in the air.

ROLL-THROUGH
Facing you,
he rolls
high wing down.

GUNS BEARING
Head on,
growing bigger
and shooting.

BREAK-AWAY
Dives—
and gets away
fast.

From a top turret . . .

[. . .] Out of range, the fighter pulls ahead of you. His far wing goes up, and for a moment he seems to hang from it as though from a hook. He then quickly swings into a head on position and starts his apparent slide. Rolling his high wing down, he moves in a straight line toward your tail. As he shifts from cone to cone, he gets bigger. He may break away above you. This gives you a momentary no deflection shot only if he appears to hang there. More often he'll roll on his back and dive away under you. [. . .]

NOSE attacks are extremely fast. Closing speeds may be 500 to 700 miles per hour. They may be made by fighters intercepting your formation or overtaking you while flying in the same direction. The enemy will fly out to the side, well out of range, until he reaches a point far ahead. After turning until he faces you, he rolls through and hurtles toward you. He may try for a few seconds to hold a pursuit curve, a little from the side, and probably high. Or he may come from dead ahead, generally almost level with you, and possibly roll over on his back as he dives under you.

Fighters ganging up like to use the nose attack. Sometimes they will line up to the side and turn in, one after another. Or they may come at you in line abreast from dead ahead. Or they may dive in pairs from high out of the sun. German fighters will often continue right through a formation trying to break it up so that they can pick off stragglers later.

★★★

20,000ft above Germany...

The June 1943 issue of Air Force *featured an article entitled "Angels Don't Shoot Guns" by Captain Bernard W. Crandell of HQ Eighth Bomber Command. In it he explained the experience of a B-17 belly turret gunner, Staff Sergeant Lee C. Gordon, or "Shorty Gordon" as he was known to the crew (on account of his 5ft 2in stature). The extract below speaks of the general environmental hostility experienced by all the crew members, flying aboard an unheated, unpressurized aircraft 20,000ft above Germany. The parachute silk scarf referred to in the passage also served as a frictionless protective barrier between the gunner's neck and the flying jacket collar; if it wasn't there, the gunner would rub his neck raw on the collar as he constantly rotated his head looking for targets:*

Preparing properly for a five-hour ride in an unheated ball turret, exposed to the full blast of the slipstream, is as important as having clean guns. For if the gunner can't take the cold, the Fortress might as well have stayed home.

What does Shorty Gordon wear on a mission? We'll start him right from scratch, from a warm G.I. cot at 0430 o'clock on a cold winter morning.

First, Shorty, you'll get dressed. Step into that clean woolen underwear and clean woolen socks and be sure they're clean because if they're not moisture will collect and freeze. Now pull on your electric suit, that one you call your "zupe suit" just because it has zippers. And the electric shoes and gloves. Next is your cotton gabardine summer flying suit, and a thin leather jacket over that. You wear RAF flying boots because they're higher than your own G.I.'s and they keep the wind—that 45-below-zero wind you found over Wilhelmshaven—off your legs. A white scarf of parachute silk to keep the heat down in your suit, and your leather helmet, and you're ready to go.

You've had a pass at the chow line now, Shorty, and here is the briefing. St. Nazaire, the U-boat base on the French coast, is your target. You know all about this one. It's the one you all say is the toughest in Europe. You've been there before. You know the story from here, Shorty, you tell it.

"I've had to clean my guns and check the turret before we take off," Shorty Gordon begins.

"When the ship gets off the ground I climb into the turret from the inside. On take-offs and landings I'm not in the turret because if we crash-landed the turret would be smashed. First thing I do is snap on the power switch, then get the guns charged. I have to charge them before we get too high because pulling back those bolts with both hands leaves me a tired guy at high altitude. When we get to the Channel I test the guns by firing a few rounds.

"The guns are pointed downward when I first climb in, but over enemy territory they are forward and low and I'm searching for enemy aircraft. If I'm in the lead ship I search to the front. Otherwise, I search to the front and side of the formation on which we're flying. If I'm in the rear element I concentrate against a rear attack.

"When the turret revolves gunners usually lose all sense of direction because they can't see the bottom of the plane unless the guns are pointing straight to the front or straight to the rear. Some of us veteran gunners can tell just what position our turret is in by the screaming of the wind. It makes different noises as the gun barrels turn in different angles. It increases in volume when the guns are pointing forward and decreases as they swing to the rear.

"As we approach the target I have to hold one hand over an earphone to be sure of hearing the others calling out the direction of attacks by enemy fighters. The wind up there is pretty bad. Besides being way below zero it makes so much noise that when my guns are firing all I can hear is 'put, put, put', and the clicking of the bolts as they go back and forth.

"When the bomb doors open I point the guns down to keep off any oil or dirt that might fly out of the bomb bay. If oil covers the sight plate I can't see to aim. I watch closely now for enemy fighters because this is a favorite time to attack.

"If I see one coming from behind the bomb bay doors I shoot right through them. It's either do that or let him get us. There is a catch on the turret that keeps the guns from swinging up and firing into the props or wings, although there have been times when our bullets have accidentally struck other planes in the formation. Luckily they caused little damage.

"When I hear 'bombs away' from the bombardier, I try to watch them falling so I can report to the Intelligence officer where they hit. On this St. Nazaire raid I watched our bombs go down until I lost them. You can't follow them all the way down when you're flying at 25,000 feet, but I estimated their direction and the time they should hit. Other bombs were hitting in the water near the target. Then I saw our first one in the water short of the target. The next one was closer, the third hit the corner of the target and the other two went right into the middle of it. There was a hell of an explosion and we found out later that we made a direct hit on a torpedo storage shed.

"There was so much flak as we approached the target that all I could see ahead was the barrage over the target, a great black cloud that hid the formation of Forts flying ahead. It was like a big thundercloud, thick enough to walk on. We all agreed later that it was the largest and most accurate barrage ever thrown up at the Forts over Europe. The barrage is a swell sight but it gets on my nerves. I could hear flak hitting the ship.

"I knew that if flak hit me while looking down I'd get it in the face, so I continued searching forward. About that time I heard someone on the interphone yell 'I'm hit,' and then another say 'I'm hit.' I thought this time we were going down in France. Everyone seemed to be shot up badly so I waited for the order to bail out. This was one mission I was wearing my chute.

"I was still searching forward when I saw the Number 1 engine on fire. I stepped on the interphone button but it was dead. I wanted to tell my pilot, Lieutenant Cunningham, about it, and wondered if I shouldn't get up into the ship and tell him. It was burning on the underside and he couldn't see it. I decided to stick in the turret because there might be more fighters coming. Finally Lieutenant Cunningham saw the fire through a flak hole in the wing and pulled the fire extinguisher on that engine. That stopped the fire, but the prop was wind-milling out of control and I was afraid it would tear off the engine.

"We were over water on the way back when I suddenly remembered that I didn't have my Mae West [life jacket] and was trying to figure out how I could get ashore after hitting the water. But then I heard someone say that enemy fighters were approaching from 11 o'clock. I ran my guns to that position, nearly straight ahead, and waited. I could hear bullets hit our ship but I couldn't see the fighters. That's one of the worst things that can happen—hearing other gunners firing but not being able to help them.

"I heard the bombardier calling out two enemy aircraft coming in low from 3 o'clock. I turned and saw them and gave the first one a long burst at 800 yards. They were Focke-Wulf 190s and one was following the other. I hit the first one. Both of them saw my tracers and started to break off. Then I gave the first one another good burst at about 600 yards and saw my tracers going into his engine. He caught fire and went into a dive. I followed him for about 5,000 feet, then started searching for the other fighter. One of the waist gunners saw the first FW splash in the water. It was easy to see because we were only at 15,000 feet. The other fighter apparently turned back.

"My feet started to hurt pretty bad when we got down to 10,000 feet because they began thawing out. I had to take off my helmet and tear at my hair to keep from feeling the pain. My electric shoes hadn't been working. That was the fifth time I froze my feet. When I search forward my feet and legs are pointing ahead, and that makes the blood run back out of them."

"The Bomber Fights Back: Power Turrets: How to Operate and Take Care of Them" was a section from a joint U.S. Navy/USAAF publication entitled The Aircrewman's Gunnery Manual, *published in May 1944. This particular section explained the construction, layout, operation, and maintenance of bomber gun ball turrets. The turrets were sophisticated pieces of combat technology, electrically powered weapons platforms that enabled the gunner to swing his weapons quickly to target and lay down fire from twin guns at a combined cyclical rate of 1,600rpm. But turrets were still difficult environments for a human being. Several miles up, the turret—which was typically not fully enclosed—would have been colder than a freezer, claustrophobically tight and uncomfortable, and oxygen starved (like all the crew, the gunners would spend most of the flight breathing from the on-board oxygen supply). Turret gunners were especially exposed to enemy fire, standing out prominently from the fuselage, while their Perspex domes gave them a terrifying all-round view of the fight to the death unfolding around them.*

From *The Aircrewman's Gunnery Manual* (1944)

Thanks to the turret . . . the bomber fights back

- Without the men who invented the turret, today's great bombing missions would be impossible. For without turrets, the bomber would be almost as helpless over enemy territory as an ordinary transport plane without a single gun.
- No one knows exactly who should get credit for inventing the modern turret. The first crude models came out in the 1920s. One was a circular mount, which the United States developed to put a little flexibility into bomber guns. The Russians tried a movable platform, cranked by hand, in which the gunner sat right out in the open, fighting the slipstream as well as the enemy.
- The modern power turret—driven by electricity and mounted inside the bomber—was developed after many experiments in the 1930s and proved its worth in action in the second year of World War II. Its effect on air strategy was spectacular. At last, the bomber–heavier and slower than the fighter plane could really fight back.
- For turrets—little blisters of Plexiglas or safety glass, bristling with caliber .50s, swinging around to meet enemy fighters no matter where they come from—enable the bomber to match the enemy slug for slug in an air battle.
- Approach an American bomber today, from any angle, and you will see a turret whose guns could be turned toward you in an instant.
- The top turret swings in a full circle; its guns move up and down from straight out to nearly straight up; it protects the whole top of the plane.
- The ball turret swings in a full circle and points its guns anywhere from straight out to straight down; it can fight off any attacker who comes from below. The tail turret throws out a big cone of fire toward the rear, and the nose or chin turret a heavy cone of fire straight ahead.
- Along with hand-held guns sticking out the waist windows and the radio position, the turrets cover almost every square inch of sky

around the bomber. No matter where the enemy fighter comes from, he must take his chances with a hail of caliber .50 bullets.

- The turrets are spun around, and the guns raised and lowered, by electric motors or by hydraulic pressure systems run by electric motors. (In the language of turrets, swinging from side to side is called moving in azimuth; up and down movement is called elevation.) All the gunner has to do is hold on to the control handles of his guns and move them to steer the turret; the mechanism does the rest.

- Inside the turret is everything the gunner needs for combat, arranged so that he can get at it in an instant. No space is wasted; although turrets are small, they have everything it takes to fight the enemy.

- As a turret gunner—no matter which turret you are assigned to—you will ride into combat seated in back of two caliber .50 machine guns and a sight. Often your seat and footrests will be adjustable; if so, learn to use the adjustments properly and you will find them a great aid to both your comfort and your efficiency.

- Armor plate or bulletproof glass will protect you as much as possible-though your best defense, like a good boxer's, will still be the offensive power packed by those caliber .50s.

- Your guns will be equipped with a special charging system—usually a pulley and cable—which makes it easy to hand charge them in the crowded space of the turret. The guns will be mounted in adapters which cushion their recoil. You will fire them by pressing triggers, usually right under your index fingers on the control handles, which release the firing pins by means of little electrical devices called *SOLENOIDS*.

- Ammunition for the guns—enough to carry you through any mission if you don't waste it—will ride in cans mounted so that the belt runs smoothly into the feedways. Often *BOOSTER MOTORS* will help lift the belt to the guns. And often the empty cases will drop through special *EJECTION CHUTES* out of the turret or into *SPENT ROUND BAGS* attached to the ends of the chutes.

- As you swing the guns around, you won't have to worry about shooting at parts of your own bomber. Every turret where this danger exists has a system of *FIRE INTERRUPTION*, or *FIRE CUTOFF*, which stops the guns automatically when they are pointed toward any part of the bomber.
- Nor will you have to worry about swinging the guns so far that they bang into your own ship. Turrets have *LIMIT STOPS* which prevent that. On some turrets the limit stops are simply bumpers; others, in addition, have automatic switches which halt the turret before any damage can be done.
- All the switches you need to operate the turret will be located within easy reach. The control handles will enable you to run the turret as easily as an automobile. Once you have developed the touch—the secret is to keep a steady hand, without jerking—you will be able to track the enemy smoothly and accurately.
- For whirling around quickly to meet a new attack, your turret will be able to get up to high speed. The distance you move the control handles will determine the speed—and in some turrets you will have a special high speed button which throws the turret into high gear to give you an extra boost. If your turret has a high speed button, use it only when you really need it—to avoid unnecessary wear and tear on the power system.
- If the turret power should ever fail, you will usually have a *MANUAL SYSTEM* for operating it by hand cranks. Some turrets even have foot pedals which enable you to fire the guns while using both hands to crank the turret into position. This is an important emergency protection; use it to keep your guns pointed at enemy fighters even though your fire cannot possibly be so accurate as when the power is on, for a motionless turret is an invitation for fighters to attack.
- Even if the guns are out of order, keep tracking the enemy; if you can't hit him, you may at least scare him away.

[. . .]

THE MARTIN UPPER

The Martin Upper is one of the most widely used of all turrets. It is designed for quick and easy operation. It has no gadgets. Everything is made for action and placed where it can be reached quickly when the chips are down.

There are several models. Some of them are improvements over old models, like a new automobile which is better than last year's. Some are simply designed for different kinds of bombers; for example, the model which goes on the B-26 is not quite the same as the one in the B-24. But if you can operate one Martin, you can operate them all.

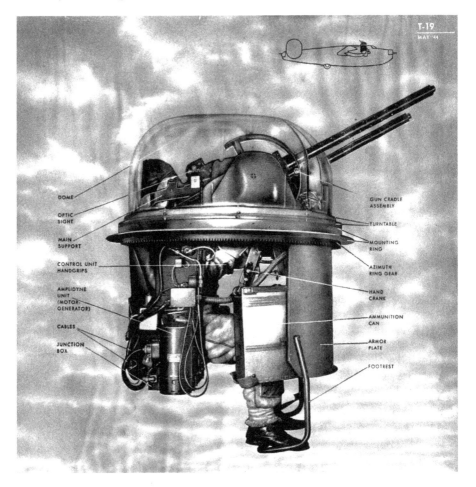

FACTS AND FIGURES

POWER

The Martin turret operates on power supplied from the bomber's central electrical system.

SIGHT

Its sight is usually the N-8 or N-6A optical. (It may also be equipped with the Sperry K-9 automatic computing sight.)

MOTION

The turret can move 360 degrees—a full circle—in azimuth. In elevation, the turret guns can be lowered and raised from a little below horizontal (−6½ degrees) to almost straight up (85 degrees).

SPEED

The turret has two speeds—normal tracking speed and high speed.

ARMOR

Armor plate is ½ inch thick. It protects the gunner in front, no matter where he aims his guns.

STOWING POSITION

The stowing position for turret and guns is 0 degrees elevation and 180 degrees azimuth—guns pointing straight back toward the tail.

Getting In

To start getting acquainted with the Martin Upper, step in. The Martin is easy to get into, simple to operate, and easy to get out of. Only one special precaution is necessary.

First turn on the main power switch—a toggle switch on the fuselage near the turret. Then adjust the footrest to fit your own height. Try it a few times to get the right position.

If you need more room to slip up into the turret, drop the bottom of the seat by pulling on the small cable stretched across the front.

Stoop and squirm up into the middle of the turret, face the front, gr the two main supports curving about your hoist your body up.

Don't pull yourself up by the sight cradle or the two nearby link rods. Your weight on the cradle may throw off the whole sight adjustment or bend the link rods and throw the sight out of line with the guns.

Finally, stand on the footrest and brace your body against the back of the seat. If you've dropped the seat, use your heel to draw it up until the latches on each side of the seat click. Sit down. Use spare seat cushions to adjust your height until your eye is level with the sight. Snap on the safety belt—and you are ready to go.

Operating the Turret

. . . where to find the controls
. . . how to use them

Close at hand, as you sit in the Martin Upper, are all the clutches, switches, and controls. They are easy to get at and easy to use-a few clicks and the turret is ready to operate. But be sure to engage the clutches and turn on the switches in the order shown here.

1

Make sure the **azimuth clutch** is engaged: the small lever, under the control handles and to the right, must be pushed **Down**. Then make sure the **elevation clutch**, a lever above the control panel and to the left, is pushed in to the engaged position to the **Left**.

2

Reach down on the right side of your seat and turn on the **master switch**. This is like the ignition switch on a car.

Never try to operate without engaging these power clutches. It is like trying to drive your car with the clutch down. You don't get anywhere, and you may wreck the turret.

3

Raise the red plastic cover on the right side of the control panel and flip on the **master gun switch**.

4

Turn the **gun selector switch** to **Both Guns**. With the switch in this position, both guns will fire when either trigger is pulled. (In the **Individual Guns** position, each gun is fired only by its own trigger. Use this only when one gun is out of action.)

5

Turn on the **sight rheostat** in the lefthand corner of the panel.
Turn it farther to adjust the brightness of the sight bulb to suit lighting conditions.

6

Finally, grasp the control handles so that the bottom edges of your hands depress the two **safety switches**. With these switches down, the turret is ready to go.

To move the turret, turn the handles just as you would steer a bicycle—to the right to go right, left to go left. Press down on the handles to raise the guns. Pull up on them to lower the guns. The slightest movement of your wrists regulates the turning, raising, or lowering.

The other controls you will need in combat are right at your fingertips. Right under your index finger on both handles are the **triggers**. On the top of the right control handle, by your thumb, is the **high speed button** that throws the turret into high speed for changing quickly from one target to another. At your left thumb is the **push-to-talk-button** that opens the interphone system for you to speak. On the main control panel are also **reset buttons** for the control unit, and booster motor circuits. Down on the front panel of your seat, behind your legs, are resets for the major electrical circuits-auxiliary power, azimuth, elevation, and firing circuits.

If you are using a gun camera, flip on the **gun camera switch** on the main control panel.

7

To charge your guns, pull cross-arm on the charger handles beside your shoulders—grasping the right handle with the left hand, and the left handle with the right hand. Pull them out sharply as far as the charger cables will go. Don't ride the cables on the return action; keep your hold on the handles but allow them to spring back under their own power.

CHAPTER 6

Flight Engineer

Flight engineers were essentially aerial mechanics who also typically served as gunners. (In the B-17, for example, the flight engineer manned the top gun turret.) Thus, they were busy individuals, supporting the rest of the crew in all manner of ways, from assisting the pilot and copilot in resolving fuel leaks and helping to control engine fires through to freeing up jammed gun turrets and lowering landing gear manually when the power supply had failed.

Flight engineers were engineers in every sense of the word. Many of the wartime manuals produced for flight engineers are impenetrable to the lay reader, replete with formulae, advanced engineering terminology, and charts packed with data. Flight engineers had to cope with an unusually broad range of structural, electrical, and mechanical systems—airframe, powerplant, hydraulics, fuel and oil systems, electrical generation and distribution, heating, oxygen supply, vacuum and de-icing systems, radios and internal communications, fire control, guns, bomb racks and release mechanisms, and more. They had to set themselves to the task of making in-flight combat repairs, regardless of the prevailing combat conditions. It is little wonder, therefore, that in the first manual extract in this chapter, from B-17: Pilot Training Manual for the Flying Fortress, *the pilot is told that "Generally, in emergencies, the engineer will be the man to whom you turn first."*

From *B-17: Pilot Training Manual for the Flying Fortress* (1944)

THE ENGINEER

Size up the man who is to be your engineer. This man is supposed to know more about the airplane you are to fly than any other member of the crew.

He has been trained in the Air Forces' highly specialized technical schools. Probably he has served some time as a crew chief. Nevertheless, there may be some inevitable blank spots in his training which you, as a pilot and airplane commander, may be able to fill in.

Think back on your own training. In many courses of instruction, you had a lot of things thrown at you from right and left. You had to concentrate on how to fly; and where your equipment was concerned you learned to rely more and more on the enlisted personnel, particularly the crew chief and the engineer, to advise you about things that were not taught to you because of lack of time and the arrangement of the training program.

Both pilot and engineer have a responsibility to work closely together to supplement and fill in the blank spots in each other's education. To be a qualified combat engineer a man must know his airplane, his engines, and his armament equipment thoroughly. This is a big responsibility: the lives of the entire crew, the safety of the equipment, the success of the mission depends upon it squarely.

He must work closely with the copilot, checking engine operation, fuel consumption, and the operation of all equipment.

He must be able to work with the bombardier, and know how to cock, lock, and load the bomb racks. It is up to you, the airplane commander, to see that he is familiar with these duties, and, if he is hazy concerning them, to have the bombardier give him special help and instruction.

He must be thoroughly familiar with the armament equipment, and know how to strip, clean, and re-assemble the guns.

He should have a general knowledge of radio equipment and be able to assist in tuning transmitters and receivers.

Your engineer should be your chief source of information concerning the airplane. He should know more about the equipment than any other crew member—yourself included.

You, in turn, are his source of information concerning flying. Bear this in mind in all your discussions with the engineer. The more complete you can make his knowledge of the reasons behind every function of the equipment, the more valuable he will be as a member of the crew. Who knows? Someday that little bit of extra knowledge in the engineer's mind may save the day in some emergency.

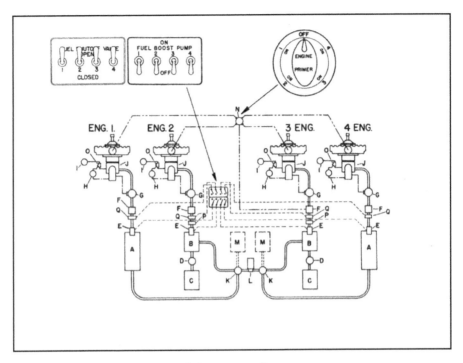

Fuel flow system diagram

Generally, in emergencies, the engineer will be the man to whom you turn first. Build up his pride, his confidence, his knowledge. Know him personally; check on the extent of his knowledge. Make him a man upon whom you can rely.

★★★

Distinguished Unit Citation for Mission to Hamm, Germany, March 4, 1943

The following unit citation, one of many awarded to the USAAF during World War II, was given on account of the efforts of the 91st Bombardment Group (Heavy) over Hamm in March 1943. The 91st flew B-17 Flying Fortresses and suffered the greatest number of losses of any heavy bombardment group, losing 187 aircraft and 887 KIA crew:

BATTLE HONORS. As authored by Executive Order 9396 (sect. I, WD Bul. 22, 1943), superseding Executive Order 9075 (sec. III, WD Bul. 11, 1942), citations of the following unit is the general order indicated are confirmed under the provisions of section IV, WD Circular 333, 1943m in the name of the President of the United States as public evidence of deserved honor and distinction. The citations read as follows:

The 1st Bombardment Division (H) is cited for extraordinary heroism, determination, and esprit de corps in action against the enemy on 4 March 1943. On this date, the 91st Bombardment Group (H) took off from home base in England, as scheduled, to attack the railroad marshalling yards located at Hamm, Germany, in one of the first operations conducted by heavy bombardment units against targets with German. This unit departed the English coast on course and a few miles out over the English Channel encountered thick haze, high cloud, and icing conditions reducing visibility to less than 1,000 yards. Weather conditions continued to deteriorate to such an extent that only the determination and skill of each pilot in maintaining formation was responsible for the negotiation of the flight across the English Channel.

Three other bombardment groups comprising the force engaged in this military operation were forced to abandon the mission because of the adverse weather encountered. Over enemy-occupied Holland, weather conditions improved and the 91st Bombardment Group (H), consisting of sixteen B-17 aircraft, continued on toward the assigned objective Vigorous attacks by enemy fighters began almost immediately. In the face of vicious opposition from an estimated 60 to 75 fighter airplanes of the German Air Force, this unit demonstrated the utmost courage and determination, fighting doggedly to maintain course and position en route to the target. Although four B-17 aircraft were lost to enemy action and heavy antiaircraft fire was met from enemy ground installations, the 91st Bombardment Group (H) successfully reached the marshalling yards at Hamm, Germany. In the face of opposition from enemy ground defenses, this unit tenaciously maintained the bomb run and bombs were dropped, inflicting extensive damage on the German installations. The 12 surviving aircraft, having successfully completed their primary assignment and having destroyed 13 enemy fighters probably destroyed 3, and damaged 4, continued to maintain formation integrity and completed the return flight to home base.

The conspicuous courage and esprit de corps exhibited by the 91st Bombardment Group (H) in the face of extremely adverse weather conditions and opposition from the enemy, which resulted in casualties consisting of 1 killed, 5 seriously wounded, and 40 missing in action, were responsible for the successful bombardment of one of the first high priority objectives assigned to bombardment forces in the European Theater of Operations. The actions of this unit reflect the highest credit on the 91st Bombardment Group (H) and the armed forces of the United States. General Orders 513, Headquarters 1st Air Division, 15 August 1945, as approved by the Commanding General. European Theater.

A B-24D Liberator flight engineer stands proudly by the side of his aircraft, *Playmate*. The antenna on the mid side of the aircraft is for the Rebecca short-range radio navigation system. (USAAF)

The following instructions for flight engineers were intended for personnel flying the Boeing B-29 Superfortress. Even today, the Superfortress has a futuristic look about it, with its slender gleaming cigar-shaped fuselage and 141ft wingspan. During World War II, however, the B-29 was truly state of the art. It featured technologies that put it in a class of its own compared to other USAAF bombers. The crew cabin was fully pressurized, meaning that the crew did not have to use external oxygen supplies, even at the B-29's service ceiling of 31,850ft. The aircraft had a General Electric Central Fire Control system that took in information from analog computer systems and allowed a single gunner to operate two or more remotely controlled gun turrets, each armed with twin .50 Browning M2 machine guns (there were four such turrets on the aircraft). At medium altitude it could carry a 12,000lb of ordnance over a 1,600-mile combat radius.

The flight engineer on the aircraft, therefore, lay his hands on the best of aviation technology. This being said, the B-29 also threw up many problems for the flight engineer to solve. The early versions of the Wright R-3350 Duplex-Cyclone radial engines, for example, had some major, and occasionally fatal, problems with reliability, especially in terms of overheating. While the manual below is specifically written for the B-29 flight engineer, many of the principles of good practice were applicable to any bomber aircraft of the war years.

From *B-29 Standard Procedures for Flight Engineers* (1944)

HEADQUARTERS SECOND AIR FORCE
Colorado Springs, Colorado
22 July 1944

1. The following B-29 check lists and procedures supersede any similar procedures for Flight Engineers. All procedures outlined herein represent the unanimous recommendations of Boeing service engineers, engine specialists, and Flight Engineers, with combat and service test experience at B-29 bases. These representatives are convinced that these approved procedures will prolong the life or the airplane, minimize accidents, and eliminate many problems of maintenance.

2. Freelance experimentation in the B-29 type airplane is hazardous and wasteful. This experimentation must stop.

3. It is therefore directed that all B-29 Flight Engineers, and instructor engineers use the following procedures as published. Criticism is encouraged and should be directed to Headquarters Second Air Force. Any changes in procedure must be approved by this headquarters before being used.

By command of Major General ENT:
ALBERT F. HEGENBERGER,
Brigadier General, General Staff Corps,
Chief of Staff

INTRODUCTION

1. The B-29 is a highly complicated, long-range, very heavy bombardment airplane, requiring the full cooperation of the entire crew to obtain the most efficient operation of this highly intricate equipment.

2. It is imperative that the Flight Engineer know his airplane. In order to accomplish this, a complete understanding of the theory, maintenance and operation of all systems of the airplane is of prime importance.

3. The Flight Engineer must be cognizant of all normal and emergency operations as set forth in T.O. 00-25-5 and Memorandum 60-10.

[. . .]

FLIGHT ENGINEER'S AMPLIFIED CHECK LIST

BEFORE STARTING ENGINES

1. Engineer's preflight
   a. Flight progress curves for both 4 and 3 engine operation.
   b. Alternate airport, considering both distance and weather conditions.
   c. Visual inspection

Don't ever assume that maintenance is perfect. Always give the airplane a thorough preflight inspection, checking the following items:

(1) Fuel tanks for servicing and proper installation of tank caps. Check fuel quantity against dip stick.
(2) Oil tanks for servicing and proper installation of caps.
(3) Turbo oil supply

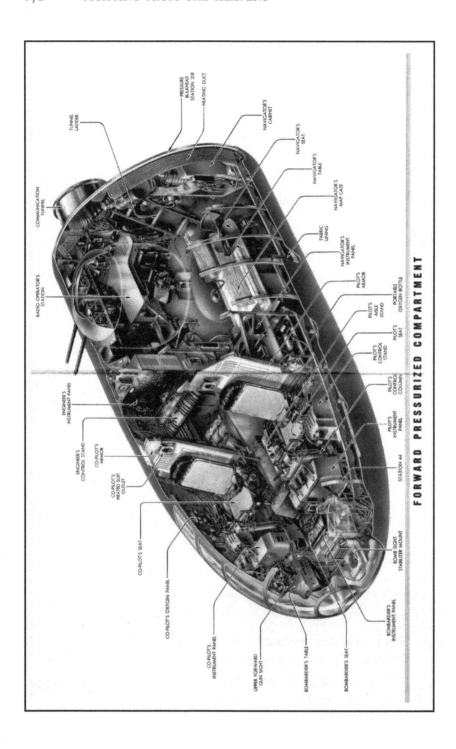

FORWARD PRESSURIZED COMPARTMENT

(4) Cowling, condition and proper fastening.

(5) Cowl flaps for proper operation.

(6) General condition of skin and control surfaces.

(7) Conditions of de-icer equipment (if applicable).

(8) Life raft doors for proper installation.

(9) All navigation or running lights.

(10) Remove air scoop seals.

(11) Engine nose sections (cracks, cylinders for condition of cooling fins and baffles, exhaust collector rings for burning).

(12) Remove pitot covers.

(13) Wheel locks removed (from older type planes).

(14) Turbo, check for cracks, binding wheels or oil leaks (in excess).

(15) Under surfaces wings and fuselage.

(16) Bomb bay, bomb racks and cannon plugs.

(17) Propellers and governors for nicks and oil leaks.

(18) Auxiliary oil tank and motor and selector valves in off position.

(19) Fuel transfer system.

(20) Auxiliary power plant for servicing and condition.

(21) Bus selector switch for normal position.

(22) All articles securely fastened.

(23) Emergency flap motor for proper installation.

(24) Bomb bay fuel tanks and selector valves.

(25) All visible cables for breaks and chafing.

(26) Axe, thermos jug, and fire extinguishers.

(27) First aid kits.

(28) Anti-icers tanks and fluid.

(29) Pressure doors closed and hinges for warping.

(30) Pressure regulator caps in up position.

(31) Tool kits installed.

(32) Oxygen equipment and pressure.

(33) Hydraulic tank for servicing.

2. Forms 1, 1A, and F

   a. Check form 1 and 1A and advise Airplane Commander of status of airplane. After entering the airplane, the Flight Engineer should go through the following check list very thoroughly.

b. Fill out loading list and Form F.

> After flying quite a few hours, all of us think we are good enough to perform our duties without the aid of a check list, but that is careless; it only takes one mistake to kill an entire crew and to completely destroy a badly needed expensive airplane. The point is: always use your check list – go through it thoroughly.

3. Parachute – check for condition.

4. Clothing – check for proper clothing for mission to be performed.

5. Life preserver – for over-water mission. Check CO_2 bottles for safety and vest for condition.

6. Battery switch – at copilot's command, put switch on.

7. Auxiliary power plant – have A.P.P. started, allow to warm up for 2–4 minutes, advance throttle, put generator switch to "run," position, put equalizer "on."

8. Emergency hydraulic pressure – check for 900–1075 PSI.

9. Hydraulic fluid – with parking brakes set and 1000 PSI, check for 2 gallon capacity.

10. Fuel booster pumps – turn pumps on, turn fuel rheostat to first notch crack mixture control and note rise in pressure, return mixture to idle cut-off.

11. Fuel transfer switches – check for "off" position.

12. Inverters – check normal and alternate inverter for 26–26½ volts, leave normal inverter "on".

13. Mixture controls – idle cut-off.

14. Throttles – open 1–1¼ inches, to obtain 900–1,200 rpm for starting.

15. Engineer's cabin air valves and pressure relief valve – closed for all ground operations.

16. Cowl flaps – flaps will be full open for all ground operations.

17. Intercoolers – full open for ground operation.

18. Oil cooler flap – check operation by putting doors to full open position, obtain position report from gunners. Close and put in automatic.

19. Pitot heat – leave in "off" position for ground operation.

20. De-icers – check for operation and leave in "off" position for take-off and landing.

21. Anti-icers – check for operation and return to "off" position.

22. Generators – switches off.

23 & 24. Fuel and oil gages – record and check against dip stick.

25. Hydraulic servicing valve – closed.

26. Oxygen – check for proper pressure and operation of A-12 regulator and blinker.

27. Lights – check for operation and spare bulbs.

28. Engineer's report – when check list is completed, inform Pilot you are ready to start engines.

BEFORE TAXIING

1. Fire extinguishers – set selector to engine being started.

2. Master ignition switch – on.

3. Start engines, 1-2-3-4
   a. Turn boost pump on.
   b. Energize 12–16 seconds.
   c. Engage starter.
   d. When prop has turned one revolution, turn ignition switch on.
   e. Prime as needed to start and smooth out engine at 800–1000 RPM.
   f. Move mixture control to auto-rich.

4. Engine instruments - check oil pressure (nose and rear), manifold pressure, RPM and oil temperature.

5. Vacuum – check for (3.8–4.2 in. Hg.)

6. Bomb bay doors closed – when copilot says, "Generators on coolest engine." Flight Engineer advances throttle on coolest engine to 1400 RPM and turns generators on. Turn generators off and retard throttle when doors are closed.

7. Engineer's report – at Copilot's request, during combat station inspection, say, "Engineer OK."

BEFORE TAKE-OFF

1. Generators – while pilot is setting throttles at 1500 RPM, have gun amplydine generator turned "on". While Pilot is checking props, turn on generators of one engine at a time. Check for voltage and amperage readings.

2. Magnetos – advance each throttle to 3000 BPM, check magnetos for RPM drop calling out to Pilot (right, both, left, both), 100 RPM maximum drop. Watch for any engine roughness.

   WARNING: Never dump throttles open as this leads to fires and backfiring.

3. Mixture controls – auto-rich. Note: Mixture controls will be in auto-rich for ground operation, take-off, climb, landing and cruise above 2100 RPM and 31 MP.

4. Fuel boost pumps – on – adjust to obtain 17 PSI plus or minus 2 PSI at take-off.

5. Report – when ready to take-off, Engineer will report to Pilot, "Ready for take-off, standing by on generators and cowl flaps."

   NOTE: If cylinder head temperature exceeds 220 deg. before take-off, idle at 700 RPM to cool, with plane headed into the wind.

6. Generators – when throttles are advanced to 1200–1500 RPM, put generators "on".

7. Cowl flaps – at start of take-off roll, set 15°, then milk cowl flaps slowly closed to obtain 7½ deg. at time wheels leave ground. CAUTION: During first third of take-off roll, carefully observe power and report any irregularities to the pilot.

8. Intercoolers – will be open on take-off and landing. With turbos off, intercoolers will be closed. At altitude or when turbos are partly on, adjust to lowest C.A.T. If icing is prevalent, obtain 25–38 deg. C.A.T.

AFTER TAKE-OFF

1. Generators – check tor amperage draw while gear and flaps are coming up.

2. Cowl flaps – adjust to maintain CHT within limits (maximum opening 10 deg. – Maximum CHT 260 deg. for take-off, 248 deg. for climb).

3. Boost pumps – when power has been reduced and 1,000 ft have been obtained, turn boost pumps off, one at a time, and observe fuel pressure.

4. Intercoolers – when turbos are turned off, close intercoolers.

CRUISE

1. When climbing, get above desired altitude, hold climb power until a speed of 210 MPH is reached. Nose the airplane down slightly, open cowl flaps to 10 deg. and maintain 210 MPH with pre-determined cruise power to cool cylinder heads. When reaching cruising altitude, level plane out and close cowl flaps to 3 deg. When airplane is on the step, adjust cowl flaps to keep cylinder head temperatures as low as possible, not higher than maximum. [. . .]

2. Intercoolers

   Turbos on, adjust as required to maintain lowest C.A.T. If icing is encountered, maintain 25–38 deg. C.

   Turbos off, intercoolers closed.

3. Mixture control – above 2100 RPM and 31" in auto-rich. At 2100, 31" and below, auto lean will be used.

   WARNING: No manual leaning from either auto lean or auto rich is to be attempted.

4. Flight log – at any major power change, or at weight change (2 hour intervals). Make entries in flight log and compute cruise control data.

   NOTE: On 3-engine operation add 11–15% fuel for auto lean, 22–25% for auto rich, to compensate for prop drag, airplane yaw and trim and added cowl flap drag.

BEFORE LANDING

1. Weight and C.G. – Engineer will compute weight and C.G. (% MAC) and give to Copilot.

2. Mixture control – put mixture in auto-rich.

3. Auxiliary power plant – start and warm up, put generator to run position and equalizer on.

4. De-icers off.

5. Anti-icers off.

6. Fuel boost pumps on.

7. Intercoolers – open for landing when turbo is put on.

8. Cowl flaps – when airspeed is slowed 175–180 to lower gear, set cowl flaps to 7½ deg. to obtain 150–160 deg. cylinder bead temperature for landing.

9. Hydraulic pressure – inform Copilot emergency pressure is 900–1075.

10. Report – inform Pilot, check list complete, ready for landing.

AFTER LANDING

1 & 2. Cowl flaps and intercoolers – upon landing, cowl flaps and intercoolers will be moved to full open position.

3. Generators – turn generators off.

4. Boost pumps – turn boost pumps off.

5. Bomb bay doors open – When Copilot says, "Generators on coolest engine", Flight Engineer sets throttle at 1400 RPM and turns generators on. When doors are open and Copilot says, "Generators Off," Flight Engineer turns off generators and retards throttle.

6. Magnetos – set throttle to 2000 BPM one at a time and check magnetos.

7. Cut engines
   a. Run engines at 700 BPM until cylinder head temperatures cool (190 deg. C., if possible). While engines are cooling at 700 RPM, flip master ignition switch to the "off" position momentarily to see that all magnetos are grounded out.
   b. Increases throttle settings to 1200 RPM and runs all engines for at least 30 sec. at this speed.
   c. Moves the mixture controls to idle cut-off.
   d. Cuts switches after propellers stop turning.
   e. Order Tail Gunner to stop put-put.

8. Switches – all switches off.

9. Wheel chocks in place.

10. Brakes off.

11. Controls locked.

A poster produced by the Office of War Information promotes the virtues of the Boeing B-17 Flying Fortress. (NARA)

12. Flight log complete.

13. Forms 1 and 1A – complete forms 1 and 1A and give to Pilot for approval.

14 & 15. Trouble shooting – Report all malfunctions to crew chief and help him locate the trouble.

EMERGENCY PROCEDURES

Landing Gear

1. Check fuse in Pilot's aisle stand. (If this fuse is burned out, both the normal landing gear switch and the landing gear transfer switch are inoperative.) Replace fuse once only and try normal gear switch again.

2. If fuse is O.K., return normal gear switch to neutral.

3. Leave landing gear transfer switch, (pilot's control stand) on normal and put bus selector switch (battery solenoid shield) on emergency with put-put on the line.

4. Then to open main doors pull emergency landing gear release handle out all the. way and hold until doors are open. The emergency gear motors, which extend and lock the landing gear, should be operated one at a time by three emergency landing gear switches – on aft wall of nose wheel well for nose gear, and on forward wall of forward bomb bay on either side of pressure door for main gear. As each emergency landing gear switch is moved to the down position, move normal gear switch to down position so that both normal and emergency motors will work together to lower gear. WARNING: If normal gear motor solenoid should be stuck in up position when using emergency procedure to lower gear, gear may extend part way then retract part way then extend part way, continuing this cycle until one motor burns out. To prevent burning out motor, instruct blister gunners to report any movement of the gear immediately. If gear should extend part way, then retract part way, turn generator switches off. Put bus selector switch on "emergency." Lower gear

with emergency switch and land. WARNING: All switches must be left in the above position until airplane has been put on jacks and solenoid replaced. A gear retraction test will be made before plane is removed from jacks. Some emergency installations include solenoid mounted above rear spar of center wing section for main gear, on aft wall of nose wheel well for nose gear. If any solenoid fails to close when using emergency landing gear switch, throw a jumper across the solenoid or close it manually.

WARNING: When using both normal and emergency gear switches, see that both are up or both down to avoid working motors against each other.

If the put-put (or battery and put-put together) is the only source of electrical power, moving the bus selector switch to emergency takes all the electric current from the normal bus. Interphone, down and locked lights, radio equipment, inverter, and all other normal equipment will be inoperative. But its engine driven generators are the only source of electrical power (both battery and put-put dead), landing gear transfer switch may be moved to emergency without taking power away from any unit except the normal landing gear switch.

5. As a last resort, to lower gear, move landing gear transfer switch to emergency. Then operate emergency gear motors as explained in number 4 above. Always transfer power first (with landing gear switch or bus selector switch), then throw emergency landing gear switch.

If main gear doors fail to open on either normal or emergency system, emergency motors will in some cases drive the gear through the doors. To avoid jamming the doors, make sure doors have had time to open all the way before operating emergency gear motors.

Tail skid does not operate on emergency system.

6. Emergency raising of gear is done in the same manner, except that main gear doors cannot be closed. Emergency motors are actuated

by the three separate emergency landing gear switches. Do not raise the gear on the emergency system if conditions are otherwise normal. Come in for a landing and see what is wrong.

WARNING: Do not practice emergency landing gear procedures. Test the equipment by means of retraction tests on the ground. Memorize the above procedures thoroughly.
CAUTION: There are no limit switches in this emergency system, therefore hold the switch in the "on" position only long enough to extend the gear. Obtain visual check from Gunners.

FLAPS

1. Flap switch neutral.

2. Put switch on top of emergency motor "down" or "up" as desired. Motor is normally stowed in flap socket in center wing section and plugged into emergency bus.

3. Lower or raise flaps as desired with landing gear transfer switch (pilot's control stand), or bus selector switch (battery solenoid shield) on "emergency." If the bus selector switch se used, put-put must be "on the line" and Tail Gunner operating the bus selector switch must return switch to normal as soon as informed (by Blister Gunners) that flaps are set as desired.

    WARNING: Do not run the motor beyond upper and lower flaps limits. This would burn out the motor, as it has no limit switch. For emergency flap operation, don't depend on the hand crank stowed forward of the rear entrance door. This crank is for starting the engines and will not fit the flap socket.

4. As a last resort, put the normal flap switch "up" or "down" as desired with the landing gear transfer switch on "normal". Then put bus selector switch on "emergency". The switch on top of emergency motor must be in the same corresponding position as the normal flap switch, or normal and emergency motors will work against each other.

A B-29 Superfortress taxis at Shemya air base, Alaska, during cold weather testing. (USGOV-PD)

OVER SPEEDING TURBOS

1. The following is recommended on take-oft or in flight for an electronic controlled turbo:
   a. Throttle back on engine.
   b. Change amplifier on turbo.
   c. If this does not remedy the trouble, then leave the amplifier cannon plug disconnected.

   NOTE: In event of runaway propeller or turbo, never feather an engine unless absolutely necessary.

[. . .]

CABIN PRESSURE

Compressed air for supercharging the fuselage compartments is supplied by the inboard turbos of the inboard engines. After compressed air passes from the impeller into the carburetor air duct, some of the compressed air is directed through the cabin air duct, through the aftercooler, and into the cabin through the cabin air valve. This happens only when the cabin air valve is open.

When the cabin air conditioning system is used, the aftercooler flap is closed to provide heat, opened to provide cooling. With the aftercooler flap closed, hot air from around the exhaust collector ring is directed through the aftercooler to heat the cabin air. With the aftercooler flap open, cool air is directed through the aftercooler, overcoming the heat of compression and reducing the temperature of air going into the cabin.

Air is released from the cabin by two automatic regulators in the rear pressurized compartment, which maintain the following cabin pressures:

> 0 to 8,000 ft. -- Pressure differential of 1 in.
> 8,000 to 10,000 ft. -- Cabin altitude 8,000 feet.
> 30,000 to 40,000 rt. -- Cabin altitude increases from 8,000 ft. to 12,000 ft.

PRESSURIZING PROCEDURE

Under normal conditions, begin pressurizing at 8,000 ft. Close all windows, pressure doors, and the cabin pressure relief valve (under left side of engineer's seat). Open the cabin air valves on the engineer's control stand.

NOTE: Be sure that knurled knobs on top of cabin pressure regulators, located at forward end of rear pressure compartment, are unscrewed, as these regulators will not operate if knobs are screwed down. When leveling out for cruising, Pilot sets up predetermined power. If cabin air flow is then too low with cabin air valves full open, Pilot will increase turbo boost slightly and retard throttles to desired manifold pressure.

Cabin air flow desired is the minimum flow which will maintain cabin altitude (see above table), but never more than 1,000 cubic feet per minute, and not more than 600 cubic feet per minute at altitudes above 33,000.

For maximum engine efficiency, set turbos to the lowest point which will maintain desired cabin air flow. If cabin pressure regulators are not working properly, screw down the knurled knobs on the cabin pressure regulators, then regulate cabin pressure with cabin air valves and cabin pressure relief valve.

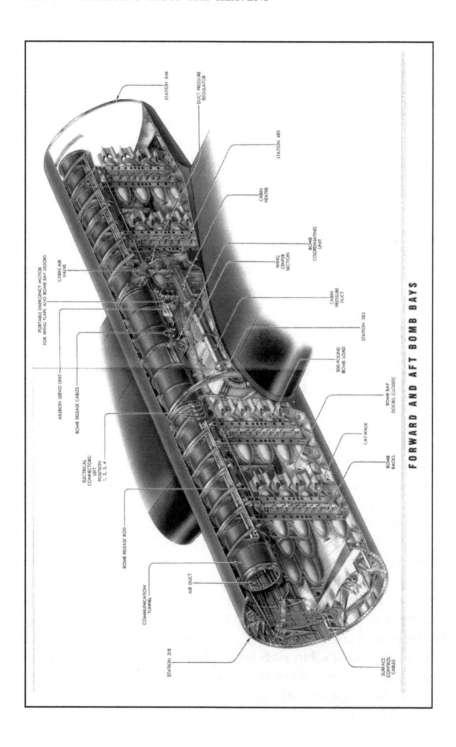

FORWARD AND AFT BOMB BAYS

STATION 646

DUCT PRESSURE REGULATOR

STATION 485

CABIN HEATER

BOMB COORDINATING UNIT

WING CENTER SECTION

CABIN PRESSURE DUCT

STATION 383

500-POUND BOMB LOAD

BOMB BAY DOORS (CLOSED)

CATWALK

BOMB RACKS

PORTABLE EMERGENCY MOTOR FOR WING FLAPS AND BOMB BAY DOORS

CABIN AIR VALVE

AILERON SERVO UNIT

BOMB RELEASE CABLES

ELECTRICAL CONNECTORS: LEFT POSITION 1, 2, 3, 4

BOMB RELEASE ROD

COMMUNICATION TUNNEL

AIR DUCT

STATION 218

SURFACE CONTROL CABLES

When operating above 30,000 feet the Flight Engineer should not allow cabin pressure differential to exceed 13.34 in. of Hq. Close cabin air valves enough to prevent higher differentials.

On all pressurized flights above 10,000 ft, Pilot will order crew members to have oxygen masks ready for instant use. Mask should always be attached to left side of helmet. If the cabin is suddenly depressurized, crew members can use oxygen immediately and prevent suffering from oxygen lack. A sudden increase in cabin altitude should not be harmful unless flying above 30,000 ft, in which case, some crew members might experience a temporary painful reaction from the "bends."

If power is set for long range or maximum endurance cruising, it may be necessary to run the inboard engines at 200 RPM higher than the outboard engines, to provide the additional boost necessary to supercharge the cabin. In this case, transfer fuel to inboard engines since they will be using more fuel. Set outboard engines at RPM which will maintain proper air speed.

When pressurizing at high altitudes, open cabin air valves slowly, adjusting these valves to a 1,000 foot per minute rate of descent. Differential pressure may sometimes seal up a leak, suddenly, during pressurizing procedure. This might push cabin rate of descent far beyond 1,000 FPM. So while pressurizing, until cabin altitude is stabilized, watch cabin rate of descent closely and be prepared to adjust cabin air valves if rate of descent changes quickly.

DEPRESSURIZING PROCEDURE

The cabin may be depressurized by closing the engineer's cabin air valves and opening the cabin pressure relief valve, if necessary. In emergencies, the cabin can be quickly depressurized by pulling either of two emergency cabin pressure release handles (Pilot's control stand, and starboard sidewall of rear pressure compartment near forward bulkhead).

Always depressurize when expecting enemy action, when ship is on fire or when preparing to abandon ship.

CHAPTER 7

Operational Challenges

We have already acknowledged the terrifying casualty rates of USAAF bomber crews during World War II. In fact, in gross numbers the USAAF suffered more casualties than the U.S. Marine Corps during the conflict. This level of attrition wasn't just about combat casualties. Flying itself was an inherently dangerous business during the war years, not least because accelerated training programs sometimes pushed men and machines beyond their limits. Some 15,000 young men, for example, died in military aviation training accidents during the war before they even graduated and had the opportunity to take an aircraft into combat. Non-combat losses from accidents—from mechanical failure, human error, severe weather, or other causes—were every bit as common as operational casualties. To the 52,173 U.S. aircrew combat deaths in World War II, we can add 25,844 deaths from accidents, half of which occurred in the continental United States. Of the 65,164 U.S. aircraft destroyed during the war, only 22,948 were due to combat—the rest were caused by a capricious range of bad luck, poor judgement, and mechanical problems, from errors in navigation through to engine fires or the catastrophic detonation of bombloads.

From a combat perspective, however, the two main threats were enemy fighter aircraft and antiaircraft fire. The Bombardier's Information File addresses the latter, explaining the various different types of antiaircraft fire that might be directed against the high-flying U.S. strategic bombing fleet. The accuracy and lethality of antiaircraft fire increased during World War II, particularly through the use of radar-controlled fire direction and aerial intercept and proximity shell fusing. The U.S. bombers, depending on their mission, might face antiaircraft threats ranging from little more than a few machine guns on pintle mounts to high-altitude heavy flak guns ringing city targets in their hundreds, each capable of firing about 15–20 rounds per minute, backed by the fighters of numerous intercept squadrons.

From *Bombardier's Information File* (1945)

FLAK ANALYSIS AND EVASIVE ACTION

To counteract the effect of AA fire, you must know the three types which you normally encounter over a target.

Continuously Pointed fire

This is the most accurate and therefore the most dangerous type of AA fire. Enemy flak gunners use it whenever they can track you and whenever your course is predictable.

It takes from 10 to 20 seconds of tracking to enable the fire control instruments to compute the lead for the first rounds and pass this initial firing data to the guns. After that, it takes from 5 to 30 seconds for the first bursts to reach your predicted position. This time of flight varies with your altitude and with the distance of the battery from your ground track. A good rule of thumb is to allow about 1 second of flight for the shell for each 1000 feet of altitude.

Once the computation of firing data has begun, the enemy guns are continuously pointed; that is, they are given a continuous lead based on your speed and direction of flight. Successive bursts then move along with the airplane or formation. One battery produces a ragged line of bursts; several batteries produce a rough cylinder of bursts.

Predicted Concentration Fire

This type of fire is delivered by several batteries operating under central control. Ordinarily it is not so effective as continuously pointed fire. But if the airplanes are free to take evasive action and are not doing so, all batteries within range may open fire with a predicted concentration. This is done to produce the maximum possible number of bursts in the formation before evasive action begins. They then switch to continuously

The nose cone of the B-17G *Nine-O-Nine*, an aircraft that survived 140 wartime combat missions. The Norden bomb sight is visible through the Plexiglas. The aircraft performed historical flights between 1986 and 2019, but was tragically destroyed in a crash on October 2, 2019, with the loss of seven lives. (Zachary Swanson/Zwanee3/PD)

pointed fire, to do as much damage as possible before the evasive action becomes effective. These tactics are frequently used at coast crossing or by itinerant or route flak, encountered on the way to or from the target.

If clouds prevent optical tracking, and countermeasures prevent accurate radar tracking, predicted concentrations or moving barrages may still be fired effectively if the formation can be followed even roughly and holds a predictable course for 90 seconds or more. If the formation holds its course for 150 seconds or more, the same guns can produce two concentrations.

Barrage Fire

This is the flak gunner's last resort. It is the least accurate type of flak and therefore the one which he least likes to use. It is expensive, too, because it expends a great amount of ammunition for a small return. When fire control equipment is missing, or if radar is completely jammed and optical tracking is impossible because of poor visibility, the flak gunners can no longer fire directly at your formation. But it is still possible for them to produce bursts where your formation may go or may be forced to go in order to bomb the objective those guns are defending. If the enemy gunners have correctly estimated your altitude and guessed the general direction of attack, they can determine roughly your approximate point of bomb release. Then the enemy can fire all his available flak guns at a point between you and your point of bomb release, in order to hang a curtain of flak you must fly through.

Flak Analysis

Flak analysis consists of determining the areas in the sky over a target where the heaviest concentration of AA fire will be encountered. It is done before a bombing mission by a trained flak analysis officer, who makes his analysis with a flak computer and a flak clock. The flak clock is a chart of known enemy gun positions protecting a specific target. In using the flak computer, the flak analysis officer considers: the maximum range of fire for each battery of guns; all possible headings for the bombing run; the total time which the bombers will spend in straight and level flight from the start of the bombing run until a few seconds after bomb release.

The flak analysis officer makes computations for each enemy battery individually and for each 30° segment around the face of the flak clock. He figures the probabilities for every gun's fire power. He takes into consideration both the course to the target and the course away from it.

When his calculations are complete, he knows the relative intensity of flak which may be expected on each possible heading. On that basis, he gives each heading a priority value.

Since his analysis considers only the vulnerability of each heading to AA fire, the flak analysis officer's findings are not conclusive in determining which heading the bombers will take on their bombing run. In planning a bombing mission all factors contributing to its success must be studied to determine the best axis of attack. Other factors which affect the bombing approach and bombing run, such as direction and speed of the wind, may be such that a 3rd instead of a 1st priority heading will be used despite the heavier flak to be expected. However, flak analysis has proven its worth by saving crews, airplanes, and equipment.

Evasive Action

There can be no established policy regarding the length of time airplanes should stay in straight and level flight over heavily defended areas or how much evasive action to take to avoid AA fire.

A certain percentage of airplanes on every bombing mission is hit by AA fire, but only rarely has a single AA burst destroyed a heavy bomber. Battle damage, however, may cause an airplane to lose its position in formation, often with disastrous results to it from enemy fighters.

Your evasive action must be planned for the area between the IP and the target. It must be planned before takeoff, so that all men participating in the bombing mission will know what is to take place and at what time.

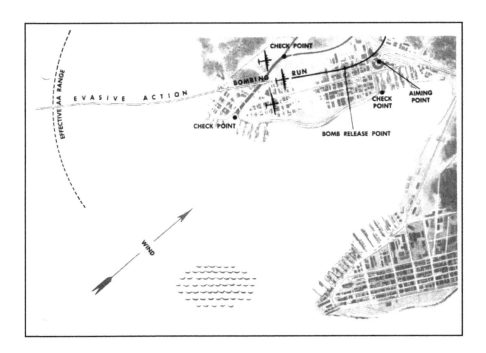

To evade AA fire an airplane can change course, altitude, or both. A change of airspeed is not conducive to maintaining good defensive formations. If in changing altitude you assume a constant glide, AA directors can compute your future position and fire accurately. You must vary your rate of descent. To be most effective, deliberate losses in altitude should vary from 500 to 2000 ft/min. That is practicable with a small formation. It is almost impossible for a large formation to attempt and still maintain a semblance of good formation.

The success of AA fire is based upon predictions. Accordingly, if you change course, the accuracy of AA is largely decreased. Changes of course should always be such that flak gunners cannot determine a mean line of flight. But always remember that extensive evasive action only prolongs your time over the target area and increases the possibility of bombing errors.

All evasive turns of the longest duration should favor the upwind direction and usually you should make 2 turns upwind to prevent S-ing. Plan to bring airplane and formation out at the proper time and on the proper heading for your bombing run.

When you fly a straight leg, alter course a sufficient time before the shell reaches your altitude to have your airplane on the original line of flight when the shell bursts. It is important to remember that when flight corrections are made the airplane does not immediately change heading. It continues on course, then gradually goes into the proper bank. The greater the airspeed the longer it takes for a correction to be applied and the airplane to assume the desired altitude.

When heavy concentrations of fire are encountered, evasive action sufficient to avoid it carries the formation too far away from the target. Experience has shown that the best way to meet a heavy AA concentration is to fly straight through it. This gives minimum time over the defended area and increases the probability of placing bombs on the target. Bombing from medium altitude presents a problem of increased accuracy in AA lire. The range of fire from enemy automatic weapons is from 0 to 10,000 feet, and although it cannot be aimed effectively above 7000 feet it adds considerably to the density of barrage type fire.

Effective evasive action on the bombing approach must be through irregular turns. The amount of turn depends upon the type of airplane flown and the size of the formation. The duration of straight legs in your evasive action should be based on your altitude and the predicted amount of AA fire to be encountered.

Summary

Good evasive action is based on these points:

1. Make your course unpredictable.
2. Make your turns slowly and smoothly. Be sure to govern the amount of turn by the size of the formation. Position the formation so that it will be on proper axis of attack at start of bombing run.
3. Make most of your turns and long legs upwind of briefed axis of attack. Know your wind and use it to your advantage. Avoid drifting downwind of your intended axis of attack and having to make your bombing run upwind.
4. Use autopilot whenever possible. Fly manually, using PDI, only as last resort. Black puffs in the sky are spent shells. Don't try to evade them. They're harmless.

★★★

Solomons Action

USAAF bomber crews were operationally dispersed across the globe during the war years, their postings ranging from rudimentary airfields in the Aleutians to well-developed bases in south-east England. A distinctive and fraught deployment came to those air crew sent to the embattled island of Guadalcanal from August to December 1942, led by B-17Es of the Seventh Air Force's 11th Heavy Bombardment Group. The following account, written by Lieutenant Hulbert Burroughs in January 1943, described how the dangers the aircrews faced were not just when airborne:

> The B-17s rolled down the Henderson Field runway early that October morning, on their way to drop a few eggs on a Jap air base at Buka and an enemy shipping concentration at Shortland Harbor. The targets were located at opposite ends of Bougainville Island.

The Zero base at Buka was visited first, and from 12,000 feet the B-17s laid a beautiful pattern of 1,000-pounders right down the middle of the runway. Five Zeros moved in to attack but they were turned back in short order.

The B-17s then turned south to Shortland and found 38 Jap ships, including battleships, cruisers and destroyers, not to mention troop and cargo transports, all gathered together for a nice bombing. The ack-ack was heavy as hell. But from about 11,000 the bombers made their runs and scored direct hits on a cruiser and a transport.

Ten Zeros came up to intercept. Two were shot down. Three B-17s collected a few routine perforations. Another was hit by a 20 mm shell that failed to explode. One of the navigators was killed by a stray 7.7 Zero bullet. A radio operator was hit in the ankle.

The B-17s turned for home. They arrived off shore near Henderson Field just as a flight of 25 Jap bombers was pounding the runway. It was easy to see that the B-17s couldn't land on the pock-marked strip, so they began circling high above the area to await developments. From their grandstand seat the B-17 boys saw quite a show.

U.S. warships near the island filled the sky with heavy antiaircraft fire. Long condensation streamers curled high in the sky as Marine Grumman fighters dived on the attackers. American landing boats in the process of unloading troop reinforcements cut the water with their white wakes as they chugged rapidly away from their mother ships.

Exploding Jap bombs kicked up huge clouds of dust and smoke on Henderson Field. Finally the bombers were driven off.

The B-17s flew low over the field but the runway had been hit twice. In a moment, however, Marine construction crews swarmed about like ants repairing the strip. Nearby a Navy dive bomber, which had been hit on the ground, sent up clouds of black smoke. Other bomb craters dotted the adjacent area.

For two hours the B-17s circled. Then, when the Marines had finished their job, the bombers landed. And just in time to get right in the middle of a repeat performance of the show they had witnessed from the air.

Within 15 minutes another wave of Jap twin-engined bombers were spotted heading toward the field. For most of the Air Force fliers, the receiving end of a bombardment was a new position. A similarly new experience was their wild scramble for Marine foxholes.

The 20 Jap bombers, flying at 20,000 feet in their usual V formation, dropped their bombs. Three hit the runway, one failing to explode. One B-17 was hit but only slight damage resulted. Most of the other bombs fell wide. Again the indefatigable Marines scrambled onto the runway and, with shovels and crowbars, trucks and rollers, repaired the damage.

By evening of that day the men were ready for a bite to eat and a night's sleep. But that's a little out of routine for Henderson Field.

At 6:30 p.m. a battery of Jap guns from the hills to the west began shelling the field. Five-inch projectiles whistled intermittently for an hour and a half. Red tracers from Marine coastal batteries rocketed back into the hills in reply. All was quiet at 9 o'clock and some of the men turned in for the night. They were optimistic.

The range of "emergencies" that might occur during a bomber mission was almost limitless in scope, but all came to the same outcome for the crew—desperate efforts to prevent the destruction of the aircraft and themselves. Sometimes the problems would emerge mercifully a short way into the flight, before the aircraft had passed over the enemy coastline or borders. In this case, as long as the pilot could keep

B-17Gs negotiate flak during a combat operation over Debrecen, Hungary. The close formation meant that the aircraft had overlapping fields of fire from their defensive armament. (FOTO:FORTEPAN / National Archives)

the aircraft flying, then the bombs could be jettisoned—over the sea, ideally—and the aircraft would return to base. In combat, however, the emergencies might come thick and fast, including engine fires, serious structural damage to flight control surfaces, key crew members killed by enemy fire, armed bombs stuck in their racks. Thousands of bomber crew died aboard their warbirds, while thousands of others were forced to make the dizzying decision to abandon the aircraft by parachute, a perilous business that often resulted in injury upon landing. Even the crews of aircraft that did make it back over home territory often faced danger, especially if they were forced to make a crash-landing on account of stuck landing gear. The following manual provides practical guidance on how the deal with a range of common emergencies.

From *Pilot's Flight Operating Instructions for the B-17F Bomber* (1942)

SECTION III   **EMERGENCY INSTRUCTIONS**

1. HAND CRANKS.

Cranks for manual operation of landing gear, wing flaps, and bomb bay doors, and for hand starting of engines, are stowed on the aft bulkhead of the radio compartment. Crank extensions for use when operating engine starters, bomb doors, and wing flaps are stowed adjacent to the cranks.

2. EMERGENCY OPERATION OF LANDING GEAR.

Each main landing gear may be operated separately by means of a hand crank connection in the bomb bay, one to the left of the door in the forward bulkhead, and one to the right. To raise one of the landing wheels, insert the crank into the connection and rotate clockwise. Turn the crank counterclockwise to lower the wheel.

DANGER
Be sure the landing gear electric switch is "OFF" before you attempt hand cranking.

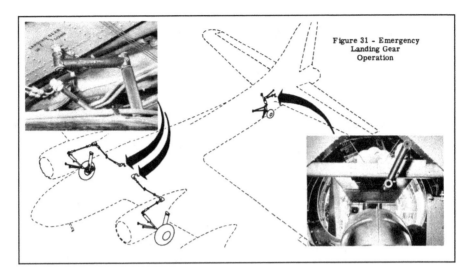

Figure 31 - Emergency
Landing Gear
Operation

3. EMERGENCY OPERATION OF THE TAIL WHEEL.

The crank used for manual operation of the landing wheels is also used for manual operation of the tail wheel. Insert the crank into the connection in the tail wheel compartment and rotate as desired.

4. EMERGENCY OPERATION OF WING FLAPS.

Lift the camera pit door in the floor of the radio compartment and insert the hand crank into the torque connection at the forward end of the pit. Rotate the crank clockwise to lower the flaps and counterclockwise to raise them.

5. EMERGENCY OPERATION OF BOMB BAY DOORS.

Insert the hand crank into the torque connection in the step at the forward end of the catwalk in the bomb bay and rotate clockwise to close the doors and counterclockwise to open them.

6. EMERGENCY BOMB RELEASE.

a.   An emergency release handle is located at the pilot's left and another at the forward end of the catwalk in the bomb bay. Pull either handle through its full travel. The first portion of the stroke releases the bomb door latches, permitting the doors to open

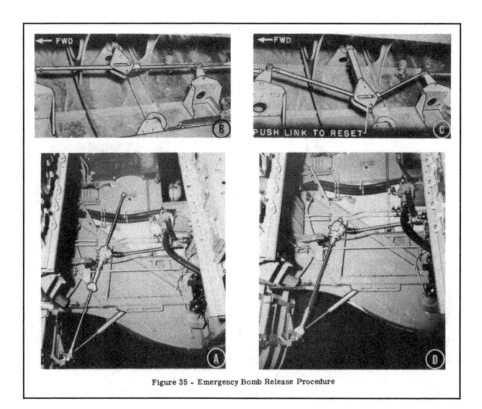

Figure 35 - Emergency Bomb Release Procedure

independently of the retracting screw. The latter portion of the stroke releases all external and internal bombs salvo and unarmed.

b. DOOR RETRACTION AFTER EMERGENCY RELEASE. If the spring in the emergency release mechanism under the hinged door beneath the pilot's compartment floor has not entirely retrieved the linkage as shown in B, reset by pushing at the hinge of the link as shown in C. Operate the retracting screws electrically (or manually) to the fully extended position. This will engage the latches between the screws and door fittings as shown in D. The doors may now be retracted in the normal manner.

7. FIRE IN FLIGHT.

In case of engine or wing fires, open the emergency exits; signal stand by to abandon: one long ring (approximately 6 seconds). In case of a

Having been hit by flak over German-occupied Serbia on April 25, 1944, a B-17F erupts into flame as its fuel tanks ignite. (USAAF)

cabin fire, exits should NOT be open; signal stand by to abandon, exits closed: one long ring (approximately 6 seconds), and one short ring (approximately 2 seconds).

 a. FUSELAGE FIRES.
  (1) Three carbon dioxide fire extinguishers are located, one on the aft bulkhead of the navigator's compartment, one on the right rear bulkhead of the pilots' compartment, and one on the forward face of bulkhead of the radio compartment.
   (a) To use; stand close to fire, raise horn, and direct gas to base of fire, holding on to rubber - insulated tubing.

WARNING

Do not grasp metal horn on top of cylinder. White discharge is "dry ice"; avoid frost bite.

(b) To shut off flow of gas, return horn to clip on side of cylinder. Extinguisher must be recharged after each use.

(2) Two carbon tetrachloride fire extinguishers are located one at the copilot's left, and one aft of the main entrance door.

(a) Stand as far as possible from the fire when using a carbon tetrachloride extinguisher; effective range is 20 to 30 feet.

(b) To operate, turn handle and pump plunger. Keep stream full and steady. To shut off, push handle in and turn until sealing plunger is depressed.

WARNING

When sprayed on a fire, carbon tetrachloride produces phosgene, an extremely poisonous gas, which can be harmful even in small amounts; and if inhaled in excessive quantities may prove fatal. Do not use in a confined area and do not stand near fire. OPEN WINDOWS AND VENTILATORS immediately after fire is extinguished

b. ENGINE FIRES DURING FLIGHT.

(1) If caused by fuel or oil leakage:

(a) Close fuel shut-off valve of engine affected.

(b) Feather propeller immediately. This stops the pumping of oil to the flames and should be done before so much oil is lost that the propeller cannot be feathered and additional damage is caused by windmilling.

(c) Slow the air speed as much as possible.

(d) Close the cowl flaps.

(e) Pull CO_2 charge (if available).

CAUTION

Leave propeller feathered. Do not attempt to restart engine while hot.

(2) Fire in exhaust due to overrich mixture:
    (a) Move mixture control to lean.
    (b) Attempt to blow out fire by engine run–up.
    (c) Close cowl flaps.
    (d) Close fuel shut-off valve to engine affected.
    (e) Pull CO_2 charge (if available).

8. EMERGENCY BRAKE OPERATION.

The emergency system operates the brake only. Pressure is applied through two hand-operated metering valves on the pilots' compartment ceiling; the left lever controls the left wheel, and the right lever controls the right wheel. If it is impossible to rebuild the pressure in the service system, use of the following procedure is recommended:

  a. Manual shut-off valve "CLOSED."
  b. Selective check valve "NORMAL."
  c. Check pressure in emergency accumulator: 650 to 800 pounds.

CAUTION
Do not attempt to raise the accumulator pressure with the hand pump.

  d. Pilot: Operate throttle and rudder.
  e. Copilot: Operate emergency brake control.

WARNING
DO NOT "PUMP" EMERGENCY BRAKES.

The pressure supply is limited and repeated applications may result in complete loss of emergency braking control.

9. WARNING SIGNALS.

The pilot can communicate with the crew by means of the interphone system, phone call lamps, and the alarm bell system. For emergency purposes, the alarm bell should be used according to prearranged signals which are thoroughly understood by the crew. A toggle switch on the pilot's electrical control panel operates three bells located, one under the navigator's table, one on the wall above the radio operator's table, and one in the tail compartment above the tail wheel boot.

10. FIRST-AID KITS.

First-aid kits are located on the bomb-sight storage box in the navigator's compartment, on the wiring diagram box on the back of the copilot's seat, and on the bulkhead forward of the lower turret.

11. ABANDONING AIRPLANE IN FLIGHT.

a. ESCAPE DOORS AND HATCHES. - All doors and hatches are quickly releasable. The side gunner's windows slide forward to open. Bomb doors may be opened by either of two emergency release handles, one at the left of the pilot and the other at the forward end of the catwalk in the bomb bay.

b. SIGNAL.
   (1) Stand by to abandon: one long ring (approximately 6 seconds).
   (2) Abandon airplane: three short rings (approximately 2 seconds each).

c. SWITCHES. - The situation will determine whether fuel and electrical systems should be turned off prior to abandoning the airplane. Under normal conditions outside of combat zones, the master ignition switch battery switches and fuel shut-off valve switches should be turned off.

12. CRASH LANDING.

a. SIGNAL.
   (1) Stand by for crash landing; by interphone.
   (2) Abandon: four short rings (approximately ½ second each).
   (3) Pilot should:
       (a) Cut engines.

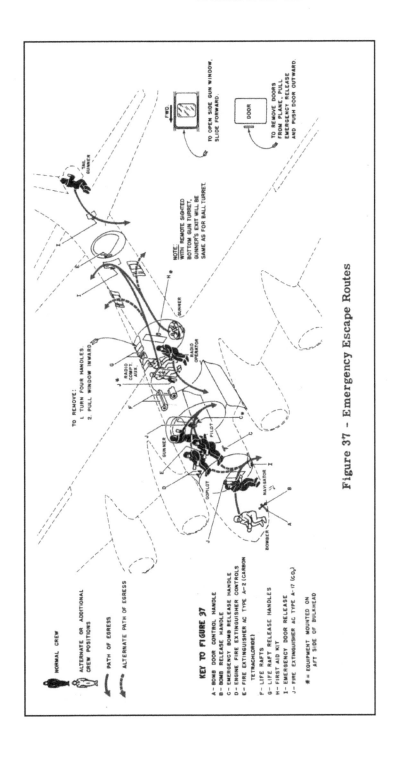

Figure 37 - Emergency Escape Routes

(b) Turn master switch "OFF."

(c) Turn battery switches "OFF."

(d) Turn fuel shut-off valve switches "OFF."

b. EGRESS.

(1) All crew members will take proper stations, remove parachutes, and fasten safety belts upon receiving interphone warning.

(2) At the signal to abandon, all crew members will leave the plane through the most practicable exit.

(3) In addition to the seven standard exits, the two side windows in the pilot's compartment are possible exits.

(4) In case some of the exits are blocked by fire, damage, or congestion, it may be best to make exit through a rupture in the fuselage, if any have occurred. Caution is required in this process to avoid fatal cuts from metal or broken glass.

(5) If there is imminent danger of fire, all personnel should disperse at least 50 feet from the airplane.

13. FORCED DESCENT AT SEA

1. As complete evacuation of the airplane should not take over 30 seconds, preflight practice drills should be participated in by all crews who are to make a flight over water, or whose operations are generally over water.

2. A complete and careful inspection of emergency equipment should be made before each long over water flight. Check life rafts, emergency kit bags (provisions), and emergency radio equipment. The kit bags and radio are stored aft of the radio compartment.

3. When it becomes evident that the airplane is to be forced down at sea due to lack of fuel, or that an altitude of at least 1,000 feet cannot be maintained, the pilot gives warning over the interphone.

WARNING!

This command must, if possible, be given while the fuel supply is still sufficient for 15 minutes of flight. The chances for a successful landing are much greater, if power is used.

4. Each crew member will acknowledge the command over the interphone.
5. The bombardier after acknowledging the command, will jettison bombs, or bomb bay tanks if more than half full, and close the bomb bay doors. If there is not sufficient time to release the bombs and close the bomb bay doors, ascertain that the bombs are "SAFE" and leave the doors closed.
6. The navigator will determine the position and inform both the pilot and the radio operator. He will take with him the instruments necessary to make simple computation while on life rafts.
7. The radio operator will jettison the hatch cover. Then, when directed by the pilot, he will send an appropriate distress signal and position. After completing this duty, he will bring the emergency radio set into the radio compartment.
8. The side gunners will jettison the side guns as they make very dangerous battering rams. If there are no side gunners, this duty should be given to other crew members before flight.
9. A crew member appointed before flight will take the emergency kit bags to the radio compartment.
10. After completing his individual duties, each member goes to the radio compartment which is the crash station for all but the pilot and copilot.
11. The pilot will direct the copilot to cut the two inboard engines, if the two outboard engines are functioning satisfactorily, and to feather their propellers.
12. Both the pilot and the copilot will strap themselves in their seats. If the side windows are to be used as exits, slide windows open, then close, insuring freedom of operation. Leave them closed until after the impact.

CAUTION!
Place axe handy in event of jamming.

13. Be sure oil emergency equipment is in the radio comportment. Throw overboard any equipment that might come loose.
14. Remove cushions from seats for head protection and take crash positions. Do not take a position in the center of the comportment

During the run-up to the Allied invasion of France, B-26 Marauders of the Ninth Air Force make a heavy daylight attack on the railway yards at Valenciennes, northern France, May 2, 1944. (U.S. Navy)

as ball turret upper structure makes this unsafe. Brace head against solid structure, if possible. Do not leave these positions until plane has come to rest as there will probably be more than one shock.

15. All members should hove life vests on, parachutes removed, and should have on all extra clothing to be worn on rafts. At night, turn off oil bright internal lights and use only the amber lamps.

16. The pilot should attempt to set the airplane down in a trough, which is usually cross wind. The two outboard engines ore used for control and to flatten the approach. The landing gear should be up, the flops lowered medium, and the ignition switches cut a foot or so above the water.

17. The water should be touched at about 90 mph. Come in as level as possible.
18. As soon as the airplane has come to rest the predesignated member will pull the life raft handles.
19. During preflight drill, men should be assigned to evacuation duties. Each man should be familiar with these so that in case of accident alternate men can carry on. Each man should know his order.
20. Pilot and copilot will exit through their side windows or through the radio compartment which before flight.

CAUTION!
No crew member should inflate his life vest until he has emerged from the airplane.

21. If the life raft is inflated upside down, one man should jump into the water and right it. If there are handling patches on bottom of raft, grasp them with both hands, and with knees on buoyancy chamber, lean back and prepare to be submerged for a moment. Even the largest raft will turn over.
22. WARNING!
Do not jump on an inverted raft, as this will expel the air trapped under it and righting becomes more difficult.
23. The rafts should be fastened together so they will not drift apart. Once aboard the rafts a check should be made to locate leaks. Repair them with the kit provided in the raft. Keep away from the airplane, if it floats but stay in the vicinity if possible. Do not remove wet clothing. Do not talk more than necessary; it dries the mouth. Do not move more than necessary; it takes energy.
24. A signal kit containing a pistol and flares is in a waterproof sealed pocket of the life raft. It may be advisable to leave the kit sealed in the pocket until a ship or a plane is sighted so as to have dry signal equipment.

Flak Danger

By January 1945, it was clear that the Allies were on course to win the war in Europe. An article written for Air Force *magazine that month, however, made it clear that there was no room for complacency in the strategic bombing campaign against Germany, especially on account of the threat from flak. Thousands of AA guns ringed Germany's cities, and flak shells downed Allied bombers in considerable numbers. A report from the Eighth Air Force Operations Section in November 1944 noted that: "During the past year enemy flak defenses have been concentrated and our bombers faced many more guns. The percentage of bombers lost to or damaged by enemy fighters has declined sharply, while the percentage lost to flak has declined only moderately. The percentage damaged by flak has remained almost constant. As a result, there has been a steady increase in the relative importance of flak until in June, July and August 1944, flak accounted for about two-thirds of the 700 bombers lost and 98 percent of the 13,000 bombers damaged." The* Air Force *article, by First Lieutenant Allan H. Gillis, was fittingly titled "They Still Have Plenty of Flak," and describes the experience of the crew aboard B-17* Lecherous Lou *against an industrial target in Germany. We pick up the action just after the aircraft had crossed over the German border:*

We had been briefed on the possibility of enemy fighter attacks and, of course, on the inevitable flak. We soon spotted the flak, but it was off to our right and slightly below us. The lazy, black, harmless-looking puffs had always fascinated me, giving me the same sort of scared thrill that a ride on a roller coaster had when I was a kid. Today I told myself we were invulnerable. After all, it was our last mission, and being shot down on our last was hardly cricket, was it? But I wasn't kidding myself. More than once, I'd seen a single burst of flak turn a powerful, throbbing four-engine plane into an enormous ball of orange flame.

For the next hour over Germany, we continued to dodge meager bursts of flak. We turned on course toward the target, and S/Sgt. Kenneth Jorgensen, waist gunner, called over the interphone:

"There's a ship in the group behind us in flames; it's spinning in!"

"Flak off our right wing," called Sergeant Crabtree.

The interphone became crowded with reports now. Two more planes behind us had been blown to bits. Both Sergeant Booker [tail gunner] and Sergeant Jorgensen reported the flak was "climbing" up to our altitude. Ahead of us and uncomfortably close, flak was bursting at our level. The bursts were large, and I knew we were getting it from the 155s. Suddenly, the flak that had been ahead of us was on all sides. The whole ship shuddered and bounced as shrapnel tore into the wings, the fuselage and the engines. I saw smoke streaming out of number one engine and flames shooting out of number three. The oil pressure on the latter was dropping, and I had just chopped back on the throttle and hit the feathering button, when hell broke loose.

Two loud reports, like a couple of 45s being shot an inch from my ear, resounded throughout the plane. Simultaneously, the Fortress was thrown up vertically on her left wing. With all our combined strength, Ross [co-pilot] and I struggled with the controls, narrowly avoiding crashing into the ship on our left. We were losing altitude fast, trying to escape the flak that was so persistently following us. Number two engine's oil pressure was almost gone and it had to be feathered. A loud hissing sounded in our ears; it was the oxygen escaping from several broken points, and we were still at 20,000 feet!

The interphone had been clear during the past three minutes, but the silence was broken abruptly by [radio operator] Ed Leitelt. His voice was steady, as if by great effort, but there were undertones of strained agony.

"Al—Joe, I've been hit in the leg—bad."

Sergeants Jorgensen and Travis [ball gunner] both rushed from the waist to administer first aid. They found the radio room full of holes and blood. Though they didn't know it at the time, Ed's leg from his knee to his ankle had been shattered to a pulp by two hundred pieces of shrapnel. Without any previous practical experience, these two men controlled the natural panicky sense of horror they felt and efficiently applied a tourniquet, gave him morphine and administered oxygen from an emergency bottle. They did this while the flak was still hammering us. One piece of German metal tore through the radio room while Sergeant Travis was applying the tourniquet and creased the side of his head, stunning him and ripping off his helmet.

Meanwhile we had dived to 15,000 feet as quickly as we dared and were doing our best to maintain it, but this was impossible with only two engines and a full bomb load. Number one engine was still smoking badly, but much as we dreaded an oil fire, we didn't dare feather it—not while we were still over Germany. First Lt. Chuck Mundorff, our navigator, had given me an approximate heading to the nearest point in Belgium and was just about to make a correction, when a burst of flak tore through the nose, smashing [bombardier] Bob O'Connell's hand and entering his left leg. The nose compartment was splattered by blood. Chuck had to administer first aid to Bob, decipher the map through the blood and figure our course at the same time.

We opened the bomb bay doors and salvoed the bombs, letting the devil take care of the Huns they killed. With this lightening of the plane, we were able to maintain a safe airspeed with a lesser rate of descent. We were still over

Germany, but with a strong tailwind favoring us, we knew we could make it into Belgium, if we could avoid further flak areas. All of us realized that a couple more well-placed shots would finish the job of tearing the plane apart.

The next 15 minutes we spent praying and cursing, praying for the sight of Belgium and cursing the Huns who made us lose precious altitude in evasive action to dodge their unexpected bursts of flak. We were at a lowly 7,000 feet, heading for Brussels, when we finally crossed the bomb line.

Brussels was our objective, mainly because we knew that there would be the best medical treatment available for Leitelt and O'Connell. However, number one engine, in addition to smoking, had begun to shoot forth flames, and it was obvious that we could never hope to make Brussels on the one remaining engine. Chuck Mundorff spotted an airfield about five miles directly ahead of us. It was only a short landing strip from which Spitfires were taking off. I could see that one end was blocked off by bomb craters, but it was here or nowhere; so we let down over the field, shooting red flares and calling the tower.

On the final approach, Chuck called over the interphone that this was the "same damn field we bombed about two months ago when the Germans held it!" Ross and I were both struck by the irony of having to sweat out crashing into our own bomb craters, and we laughed—in a rather high-pitched way. We set the wheels down on the very edge of the runway and brought Lou to a brake-burning, screaming halt about 15 feet from the nearest crater.

There was an ambulance waiting, and by the time we had cut the two engines, the medics were inside the ship getting out Ed. Bob came out under his own locomotion, protesting that he had nothing but a scratch. He almost collapsed under the strain of trying to convince us, and the medics bustled him into the ambulance.

We were all pretty glum during the interrogation. Ed had been unconscious for a half-hour before landing and no one knew just how close to death he might be. As soon as the formalities were over, we raced to the field hospital where he had been given emergency treatment. The medical officer assured us that though Ed's condition was serious, he would live. The wave of relief that ran through us was almost tangible.

Lecherous Lou was a sad-looking sight; she'd given her all that day. As we hauled our equipment out of her guts, we knew from now on she would be a ground-stomping spare- parts depot. It was sad, but she had brought us home from our toughest mission and our last. She had done her job, and we had done ours, and we left her there on the muddy airstrip, a gallant and tired old girl.

Sources

Bibliographic information refers to the sources of both text and images.

Chapter 1: Recruitment and Training

USAAF, *Aviation Cadet Training for the Army Air Forces* (Washington, D.C.: Headquarters, AAF, 1943)

Brown, Captain V. W., "Confessions of a Veteran Pilot," *Air Force* (June 1942)

Chapter 2: Pilot and Copilot

USAAF, *Pilot Training Manual for the B-24 Liberator* (Washington, D.C.: Headquarters, AAF, Office of Flying Safety, 1945)

USAAF, *Pilot Training Manual for the Mitchell Bomber B-25* (Washington, D.C.: Headquarters, AAF, Office of Flying Safety, 1945)

USAAF, *B-17: Pilot Training Manual for the Flying Fortress* (Washington, D.C.: Headquarters, AAF, Office of Flying Safety, 1944)

Head, Second Lieutenant Ivan P., "Tactical Study of Attack on Convoy Near Lae, New Guinea" (March 10, 1943)

Maginnis, First Lieutenant James J., "Positionality—A Straggler," *Air Force* (November 1943)

Chapter 3: Bombardier

USAAF, *Pilot Training Manual for the B-24 Liberator* (Washington, D.C.: Headquarters, AAF, Office of Flying Safety, 1945)

War Department, *Bombardier's Information File* (Washington, D.C.: War Department/ Headquarters, AAF, 1944)

Armstrong, Brigadier General Frank A., Jr., "Air Discipline," *Air Force* (November 1943)

Chapter 4: Navigator and Radio Operator

USAAF, *Pilot Training Manual for the B-24 Liberator* (Washington, D.C.: Headquarters, AAF, Office of Flying Safety, 1945)

XX Bomber Command, *Combat Crew Manual: XX Bomber Command APO 493* (Marianas: XX Bomber Command, 1944)

USAAF, *Familiarization and Maintenance Manual for the B-29 Bomber* (Dayton, Ohio: Materiel Command Wright Field, 1944)

Gordon, Major Arthur, "'Flying Submarine,'" *Air Force* (May 1944)

"Last Flight," *Air Force* (November 1943)

Chapter 5: Gunners

USAAF, *Gunner's Information File—Flexible Gunnery* (Washington, D.C.: Training Aids Division, Office of the Assistant Chief of Air Staff, HQ AAF, 1944)

U.S. Navy/USAAF, *Aircrewman's Gunnery Manual* (Washington, D.C.: Aviation Training Division, Office of the Chief of Naval Operations, U.S. Navy, in collaboration with U.S. Army Air Forces, 1944)

Cranwell, Captain Bernard W., "Angels Don't Shoot Guns," *Air Force* (June 1943)

Chapter 6: Flight Engineer

USAAF, *B-17: Pilot Training Manual for the Flying Fortress* (Washington, D.C.: Headquarters, AAF, Office of Flying Safety, 1944)

Second Air Force, *B-29 Standard Procedures for Flight Engineers* (Colorado Springs, Colorado: 2AF, 1944)

USAAF, *Familiarization and Maintenance Manual for the B-29 Bomber* (Dayton, Ohio: Materiel Command Wright Field, 1944)

Distinguished Unit Citation for Mission to Hamm, Germany, March 4, 1943

Chapter 7: Operational Challenges

War Department, *Bombardier's Information File* (Washington, D.C.: War Department/ Headquarters, AAF, 1944)

USAAF, *Pilot's Flight Operating Instructions for the B-17F Bomber* (Washington, D.C.: Commanding General, Army Air Forces, the Chief of the Bureau of Aeronautics, and the Air Council of the United Kingdom, 1942)

Burroughs, Lieutenant Hulbert, "Air Forces Action in the Solomons," *Air Force* (January 1943)

Gillis, First Lieutenant Allan H., "They Still Have Plenty of Flak," *Air Force* (January 1945)